NEW EDITION, REVISED AND ENLARGED

A TREATISE
ON
HARMONY

WITH EXERCISES

By

J. HUMFREY ANGER

Professor of Harmony, etc., at the Toronto Conservatory of Music;
Hon. Mus. Doc., Trinity University, Toronto;
Mus. Bac., Oxon.; F. R. C. O.

In Three Parts

PART I

$1.25

Boston, Mass.
THE BOSTON MUSIC COMPANY
G. Schirmer, Jr.

PREFACE.

It has been the privilege of the author to teach the theory of music, and *nothing but the theory*, for the past ten years. During this extended period he has naturally had exceptional opportunities for discovering the difficulties which confront the average student; and the special purpose of this present work, the outcome of many requests from both past and present pupils, as well as from fellow teachers, is to assist the student to meet and master these difficulties, so that Harmony, which is one of the most important and, at the same time, one of the most charming studies in the art of music, may become a source of pleasure and enjoyment, instead of being, as so frequently happens, a source of worry and annoyance.

The author has endeavoured, in his treatment of the subject, to be as *simple*, as *concise*, and at the same time as *thorough* as possible; simplicity being a necessity for the beginner in every subject; conciseness, a necessity at the present day, when harmony is but one of the many studies which claim the attention of the student; while a thorough explanation of the subject is not only absolutely necessary, but this, indeed, must also be on somewhat original lines in order to justify the publication of yet another work on a subject upon which so many excellent treatises have already been written.

It is not to be supposed, however, that any very original theories will be advanced in the early chapters of the present work; on the contrary, the author is convinced that *the first object* of the student should be to acquire a perfect knowledge, as far as possible, of that purity of harmonic structure upon which the immortal compositions of a Mozart were based. The modern composer, to whom a new effect is always an object to be attained—for the feeble platitude and the dishonesty of plagiarism should ever be avoided—will discover almost endless possibilities in the modifications of the chords in general use, either by the employment of auxiliary notes, or by the introduction of the chromatic element. Whatever originality there may be in the present work will be found, therefore, in a later chapter, wherein the author, in order to meet the requirements of modern composers, advocates the adoption of a new scale (see Ex. 5, page xi), the principal feature of which is the combination of the enharmonic element with the already accepted chromatic extension of the major scale.

Considerable attention has been devoted, throughout this work, to the exercises at the end of each chapter. These, it will be seen, are both numerous and of a *varied* character. In addition to figured basses, which may be regarded as the staple form of exercise, there are also exercises on the analysis of chords, on the introduction (including the preparation and resolution) of discords, on the harmonization of melodies and unfigured basses, on clothing blank rhythms with harmony, and on composing original passages, etc. In all cases the exercises have been carefully *graded*, and have been arranged with the special view of assisting candidates preparing for examinations. The student, however, is not necessarily expected to work all the exercises at the end of each chapter; many of them being of a suggestive character, may, at the discretion of the teacher, be omitted, or on the other hand, others of a similar type may be added either by the teacher or by the student himself.

It seems to be a moot question as to whether the student should, or should not, be taught to harmonize melodies from the beginning. The author is inclined to think not, but everything really depends on the student; for though one student will grasp the principles readily enough, and another will fail to do so, both of them may in the end prove to be equally successful in their general work. This matter must also be left with the teacher, and if the exercises on harmonizing melodies, etc., are omitted when the chapter is first studied, they will probably be found useful in review work at a later day.

Another feature, and one to which the author attaches much importance, is a system by which both *time* and *space* may be saved in writing the names of chords. By the use of the signs, + for major, – for minor, o for diminished, and × for augmented, combined with certain Roman and Arabic numerals, each chord may be designated by means of a symbol (somewhat resembling the symbols used in Chemistry), placed below the bass-note. The saving in time and space will be readily seen from one or two examples, thus :

SYMBOL.   SIGNIFICATION.

V_7^1 The first inversion of the dominant seventh.

$I{-}^2$ The second inversion of the tonic minor common chord.

$\times IV_7 o$ The diminished seventh on the chromatically raised subdominant.

Suspensions, and in fact every chord employed in music, may also be represented. In no case, it may be said, is the generally accepted system of figures (employed for the figured bass), tampered with.

In this symbol system, which is explained in Appendix 1, the first six notes of the scale are represented by the first six Roman numerals, the Leading note, however, is represented by the letter L, in order that the attention of the student may more readily be directed to the characteristics of this note, which not only has, as a rule, a fixed progression, but which, unlike the other notes of the major scale, is never the root of a diatonic common chord, and never the tonic of an attendant key. The minor seventh in the minor scale will be known as the subtonic, in preference to the somewhat awkward expression, "flattened leading-note," and is represented by the Roman numeral VII. This system, it is hoped, will supply a long-felt want, for instead of regarding the analysis of chords as a somewhat irksome task, the earnest student it has been found, takes a delight in trying to discover the correct symbols for the various chords as they occur in an exercise.

Another feature of this work, to which the author would draw attention, is the theory of the best treble note. In certain chords, such as the sixth on the subdominant, the cadential $\frac{6}{4}$, the second inversion of the dominant seventh, etc., one note in particular is often preferable in the treble, and this note has been pointed out in every instance. In no case, however, is the treble note for the *first* chord of an exercise suggested by the use of a figure below the bass note; a plan which, while frequently adopted in text books, savors, in the opinion of the author, of mistaken kindness. Before commencing to work a figured bass the student will do well to jot in here and there, wherever possible, the best treble notes, especially at the cadences; these will not only become *stepping stones*, as it were, and so prevent that aimless groping in the dark, so common with beginners, but will also, as a rule, ensure *an interesting melody*, a feature often lacking in an otherwise correct exercise.

The leading and diminished seventh chords are treated as being derived, respectively, from the dominant major and minor ninth chords, by *the omission of the dominant*, but in neither case is the chord called the first inversion of the dominant ninth; the student being taught that in the last named chord the dominant is *always* present, while in the chords of the seventh on the leading note the dominant is *never* present. A distinction is thus made where a difference, if perhaps only a slight one, certainly seems to exist.

In the treatment of suspensions the author teaches that *the concord is the suspended note*, the discord being the *suspending* note; for it is the concord over which there is suspense while the discord is being heard.

Thus, in the suspension 9 to 8, the ninth is the suspending note, and the octave the suspended note, the ninth and the octave together, of course, constituting the suspension. Suspensions are also taught as being of two kinds, *rising and falling*, so that the term 'retardation' is unnecessary in this connection; a suspension is always regarded as falling unless the word *rising* is used, in the same way that a scale is always regarded as being major unless the word *minor* is used. The term 'retardation' is employed for the so-called 'driving notes,' and is considered in conjunction with the 'anticipation,' of which it may be regarded as the converse.

    Secondary sevenths are treated under this heading of *fundamental discords*; a fundamental discord being regarded as a discord derived from a fundamental note or root. Thus, the chord at *a*, **Ex. 1.** Ex. 1, in the key of C, is the *supertonic seventh*, II7; in the key of B-flat this same chord would be the *mediant seventh*, III7. The chromatic chord at *b*, in the key of C, is the *primary seventh on the supertonic*, II+7. In each case the root is the same, viz. D. The seventh on the dominant, though regarded as a primary seventh, is always called a dominant seventh.

    Much attention has also been devoted to the subject of **harmonic progressions.** The best progressions both to and from the various chords, as they severally occur, are considered in every instance, so that the student may learn to write short passages, introducing given chords; ability to do which is now necessary in theoretical examinations.

    The **line of continuation** is used to indicate the retention of one or more notes from the *preceding* chord; this, the original meaning of the term, avoids all confusion, and avoids also the necessity of adding a mark (of any kind whatever) to the bass-note of a common chord.

    The **illustrations** throughout this work have been given in the keys of C major and either A or C minor, but they should in every case be transposed into other keys, and the more important examples should be *committed to memory.*

    No illustrations from the compositions of the great masters have been included, for though of considerable interest to the true musician, it is a question whether such examples are really of any benefit to the student. Speaking generally, it may be said, that for every example chosen to prove a rule, another example could probably be found, possibly in the works of the same composer, which might be quoted to disprove the rule; indeed, to furnish adequate illustrations, with exceptions, and explanations, a work on harmony would become an extremely bulky volume, far exceeding both the intentions of the author and the limits of the present work.

In order to avoid unwieldly dimensions, this treatise has been divided into three parts, the contents of which may be summarized as follows :—

PART I. The major and minor diatonic scales, intervals, the common chord and its inversions, cadences, sequences, the dominant seventh, and natural modulation.

PART II. Secondary sevenths, the dominant ninth with its derivatives—the leading and diminished sevenths, suspensions, auxiliary notes, and extraneous modulation.

PART III. Chromatic concords and discords, enharmonic modulation, certain modified chords, harmony in other than four parts, contrapuntal part writing, and the string quartet.

No mention, it will be seen, is made in the above synopsis, of chords of the eleventh and thirteenth. To this theory of chord construction the author is *altogether opposed*, though at the same time fully appreciating the great work which Alfred Day, M.D. (1810-1849), the originator of the theory, accomplished for the advancement of the art, and fully recognizing also the strong support which it has received at the hands of many of the most eminent theorists in England and America.

Bach, to whom we are indebted for the establishment of **equal temperament**, *the very basis of all modern music*, died practically a hundred years before the Day theory was promulgated. Moreover, to Beethoven, the acknowledged greatest musical genius the world has ever seen, this theory was absolutely unknown. The student, therefore, who would examine and study the works of the great classical masters, will find the Day theory, to say the least, unnecessary. Furthermore, it cannot so much as be assumed that the great composers wrote, even unconsciously, in accordance with this theory, for the notation of certain chords which occur in their works, Ex. 2. is entirely at variance with this theory. The chord at *a*, Ex. 2, for instance, is *disallowed*, and when thus written, the D-sharp is said to be 'incorrect notation employed for convenience,' and should, it is claimed, be E-flat, as at *b*; the chord being, according to the Day theory, the dominant minor thirteenth, and the two chords being *one and the same chord*. According to the theory advocated by the author, the chords are *not the same*; that at *a* is the $V^7_{6\times}$ *i.e.* the dominant seventh with the fifth augmented, in the key of C major; while the chord at *b* is the V^7_{6-} *i.e.* the dominant minor sixth and seventh, in the key of C minor. This chord, it may be said, will be explained in due course, and the name, which at first may appear somewhat strange, will, it is felt, be justified by the explanation.

Here then are two conflicting theories. In the one case, the two chords are regarded as being the same, and the composer, whoever he be, that writes D-sharp, is wrong; in the other, the chords are different, with different symbols and names, in different keys, and even possess, as will be shown below, different effects, while the composer may write whichever his fancy dictates. The fact that these chords are identically the same on the piano is *no proof whatever* in favor of the Day theory, for this may also be said of the German form of the augmented sixth, which is identically the same on the piano as the dominant seventh; and the same may also be said of the various enharmonic changes of the diminished seventh, but no incorrect notation is claimed for these chords.

The difference in the **mental effect** of the chords at *a* and *b*, to which reference was made above, is due in part to the difference between G to D sharp, which is an augmented fifth, and G to E flat, which is a minor sixth; in the latter case the interval is *consonant*, in the former, it is *dissonant*. This difference in effect will be readily appreciated if the natural resolutions of these chords, shown at *a* and *b*, Ex. 3, are played on the piano. The progression at *a* is tinged with *joy*, that at *b* with *sorrow*. A veritable illustration of musical antithesis. Now, effects such as these are as readily appreciated with the *eye* as with the *ear* by the true musician. Beethoven, it is well known, composed his

Ex. 3.

greatest works whilst suffering from total deafness. He, with the eye alone, could appreciate the majestic harmonies of the 'Choral Symphony.' It is therefore hardly right to suppose that the great masters wrote one thing and intended another; and it is hardly just to claim that they heedlessly or needlessly sacrificed *correct* notation for *convenient* notation. Examples of incorrect notation may perhaps occur occasionally, but they are very rare indeed in the works of the best composers; even the well-known pre-cadential chord in the Andante of Beethoven's 'Sonata appassionata' (measure 6), in which the consecutive fifths are hidden from the eye, only by the notation employed, can be explained, and the composer absolved from the sin of incorrect notation.

It may be claimed that certain chords can only be explained as chords of the eleventh or thirteenth ; to this the author would lay a counter-claim, that such chords do not exist in the works of Bach, of Beethoven, or indeed of any of the old masters ; for surely these great composers wrote in accordance with *some* theory, and it has been shown that this was *not the Day theory.* Furthermore, this theory is even more inadequate when applied to modern compositions ; for C-sharp is employed as freely as D-flat, D-sharp as E-flat, and G-sharp as A-flat, in the key of C major at the present day. The old cry of 'incorrect notation' is no longer plausible ; it is little short of an insult to the good composer; and the day has now come when *the theorist must be prepared to account for all such* chromatic progressions.

A modern author * of a valuable work on harmony, says that he bases his system "on the Diatonic, Chromatic and Enharmonic scales, and ventures to prophesy that the Text-book of the future must and will follow some such plan, in order consistently to explain modern combinations, which, under the theoretical systems at present in vogue, require a wrong application of the laws of acoustics, and a complex multiplication of roots." With these sentiments the author of the present work is in perfect accord, and the theory which he advances to meet these modern requirements will be propounded in Part III of this work. Here it will be shown that the complete key of C major, the *materiel*, so to say, at the command of the composer, may be obtained by the formation of **a series of primary ninths**, commencing, like the Day theory, with the tonic as the original generator of the key; this is followed by a primary ninth on the dominant, as the fifth of the tonic ; and this, by another on the supertonic, as the fifth of the dominant. So far this is *in keeping with the Day theory.* "The reason," to quote Dr. Day's own words, " why the tonic, dominant, and supertonic are chosen for roots, is because the harmonics in nature rise in the same manner; first the harmonics of any given note, then those of its fifth or dominant, then those of the fifth of that dominant, being the second or supertonic of the original note. The reason," and to this the author would draw *particular* attention, "why the harmonics of the next fifth are not used is, because that note itself is not a note of the diatonic scale, being a little too sharp (as the fifth of the supertonic), and can only be used as a part of a chromatic chord." The latter part of this quotation may be, and is,

---

*Dr. Charles Vincent, author of "Harmony, Diatonic and Chromatic." The theories on the origin of the Chromatic element in modern music, advocated in the present work, differ considerably, however, from those of Dr. Vincent.

perfectly true from the standpoint of acoustics; but *acoustics and equal temperament are by no means one and the same thing*. B-flat, for example, as the minor seventh of C, is also out of tune (again a little too sharp,) with B flat the seventh harmonic of the generator C, nevertheless it is the *out-of-tune* note which is employed in equal temperament ; and again, even the major third of art is not *perfectly* in tune with the major third of nature.

Another, and an interesting illustration of this point will be seen in the major and minor tones. The interval between the first and second degrees of the major scale, is a major tone, with the vibration ratio of 8 to 9, while the interval between the second and third degrees is a minor tone, with the ratio of 9 to 10. Now the first and second degrees in the key of D, for example, are exactly the same, *according to the laws of equal temperament*, as the second and third degrees in the key of C ; wherefore, if the note D has, say, 288 vibrations, then the note E, in the key of D, will have 324 vibrations, whereas in the key of C this selfsame note, E, will have only 320 vibrations. Theoretically this is a fact, practically it is absurd. The difference between theory and practice in this and in similar instances, may be explained on the grounds, that the demands of equality in art have necessitated the sacrifice of inequality in science. Even supposing that the violinist and the vocalist can exemplify the difference between the major and the minor tone, the effect would not be in accordance with the principles upon which the modern major diatonic scale is constructed ; for the fundamental principle of this construction is equality, the octave being divided into twelve mathematically *equal* semitones.

In the old meantone, or unequal temperament system, the semitones were *not all equal*, with the result that certain keys, called "wolves," could not be employed at all ; when, therefore, the 'Wohltemperirtes Klavier', in which there are preludes and fugues in *every* key, made its appearance, the old system gradually passed away, and equal temperament *became*, and has *since remained*, the definitely established system.

Returning now to the point in question, since all the *semitones* are exactly equal, it follows that all the perfect fifths will *also be equal*, and equal in every respect, for it is upon this very principle that the modern system of scale construction is based, every new scale being the exact counterpart of the last, exact in every particular except that of pitch alone. It will, therefore, be seen that the fifth of the supertonic, which Dr. Day states is "a little too sharp," cannot be *the same note* as that which is employed for the submediant in the modern major scale, *all the fifths in which are equal.*

It was then this very question of **perfect equality** which prompted the author to continue the series of primary ninths from the point at which Dr. Day ends. For, since the fifths are all equal, the submediant will be in the same relation to the supertonic as the supertonic is to the dominant, and as the dominant is to the tonic. Having, therefore, formed chords of the primary minor ninth upon the tonic, the dominant and the supertonic, *the* **submediant** *is taken for the next chord*, after which the **mediant** is taken, and finally the **leading note**; finally, because the perfect fifth above the leading note can *never form part* of a diatonic scale. A series of chords is thus obtained, the natural evolution of which, from the original tonic as a generator, will be seen in the following example :—

Ex. 4.

The whole notes in the above example are the roots of the successive chords; the quarter notes, in each case, form a chord of the diminished seventh. These chords, it will be seen, extend over a compass of exactly four octaves, commencing and ending on the tonic of the key.

A **scale** may now be formed from the notes comprised by these chords, a scale which the author believes will meet all the requirements of the modern composer, a scale containing not only the diatonic and the chromatic, but also the **enharmonic** element, and which may therefore be termed

Ex. 5.   The Modern Enharmonic Scale of C.

The half notes in the above example are the diatonic notes of the scale; the quarter notes are chromatic, and are called the **perfect chromatics**, being diatonic to the attendant keys they are never enharmonically changed; the eighth notes are called the **imperfect chromatics** and may be employed in either form.

If this scale then is taken as the basis for all the possible chords in the key of C major, **three important new triads**, viz., A major, E major and B major, besides others, are added to the already accepted chromatic concords. These, it will be seen, are the dominant triads of the three attendant minor keys, and by their acceptance the whole family of attendant keys becomes even more closely united with the original tonic key than heretofore. By the addition of these triads, together with their sevenths and ninths, **a theory of harmony** is obtained by which *every chord* in the works of the great composers can be *justified*. Furthermore, the modern composer will find at his command a major triad on every semitonal degree of the key, except alone on F-sharp (or G-flat), which, having no note common to the diatonic scale, is naturally altogether foreign to the key. At the same time, **seemingly boundless possibilities in the realm of tone color** are presented to the composer, possibilities which indeed may *never be exhausted* so long as the art of music is based upon these very principles of **equal temperament.**

The chief defects of the Day theory may be briefly summarized as follows :—

(1) It was altogether *unknown* to the great classical masters of the **Bach to Beethoven** period (and even later); indeed, it frequently happens that chords employed by these composers cannot be explained by the Day theory, in which case the chords are said to be written in *False notation.*

(2) The *compound* intervals of the eleventh and thirteenth being represented in figured basses by their *simple* forms—the fourth and sixth, the names 'dominant fourth and dominant sixth' are just as applicable and quite as justifiable as the names 'dominant eleventh and thirteenth.'

(3) These names, furthermore, are very **indefinite.** Dr. Day furnishes *thirty-two* different examples of the use of the dominant eleventh, and as many as *seventy* different examples of the use of the dominant thirteenth.

(4) The theory completely overthrows the generally accepted theory of **roots,** and, consequently, **root progressions,** for any diatonic triad or chord of the seventh may be regarded as an *incomplete form* of the dominant thirteenth.

(5) The **harmonic form of the chromatic scale** being the basis of this theory, and this scale being derivable from the chords of the *ninth* on the tonic, dominant and supertonic, *nothing is gained* by adding the eleventh and thirteenth to these generators.

(6) It is founded (as has been shown above) upon a false estimate of the true significance of **equal temperament,** in which, for the purpose

of enharmonic changes, all the semitones—whether diatonic or chromatic—must be regarded as being *absolutely equal.*

(7) Finally, when applied to the works of the great modern composers—Wagner, and his contemporaries and successors, this theory *signally fails,* for, in the chromatic extension of the modes now in vogue, a primary seventh, (to mention one chord alone) may be employed not only upon the tonic, the dominant and the supertonic—as advocated by Dr. Day—but also upon *all the degrees* of the major scale.

The various theories of harmony, however, after all is said and done, may well be likened to the different paths up mount Parnassus. The originator of a theory is simply the discoverer of a new path, the teacher is the guide, and the student is the pilgrim. To reach the summit is the object of all. Are we not but too frequently prone to believe that the path we ourselves trod is the only path? May not the pilgrim occasionally take another path? Should not the guide be acquainted with every path? Is it not the part of the discoverer to find, if possible, the smoothest path, to remove obstructions and to grade the road where necessary, and thus to prepare a way which from his heart he feels will be welcomed by all? A path of joy to the guide, a path of comfort to the pilgrim.

To all his pupils, past as well as present, the author dedicates this work ; and if it be the means of elevating their musical taste, or the means of arousing a keener desire for, and a better appreciation of, the higher types of music, or the means of leading them into the realm of composition, when perhaps they may add something, if only a small contribution, to that wealth of music of which we are already the happy possessors, then indeed will he feel repaid, and amply repaid, for the time and labor spent upon the same.

To his friend and pupil, Mr. Edmund Hardy, Mus. Bac., for valuable assistance in reading proofs, the acknowledgments of the author are due, and are cordially tendered.

TORONTO, CANADA,
August, 1903.

TABLE OF CONTENTS.

PART I.

The titles of the above chapters refer to the *principal* subjects under treatment in the various chapters; other cognate subjects, however, are often introduced, as in chapter III, where a brief reference is made to the chromatic scale; and again in Chapter VI, where the principle of modulation is explained, and reference is made to the 'Additional triads' of the minor mode.

A TREATISE ON HARMONY

INTRODUCTION.

THE period at which Harmony first began to be an important factor in music appears to have been about the end of the sixteenth century, being contemporaneous with the establishment of the modern diatonic scales, with the gradual development of Form in musical composition, and with the rise of the opera and oratorio, all of which are the direct results of the Renaissance, the period therefore in which modern music had its birth.

Prior to this period, all music was composed on a basis of Counterpoint. Counterpoint was, and is, the art of combining two or more melodies The first school of contrapuntal composers arose in the fourteenth century, and before this era Harmony, as we understand it, did not exist.

In Harmony, music is regarded from the perpendicular point of view; in Counterpoint, from the horizontal. The highest types of modern classical music may be said to be built upon a union of Harmony and Counterpoint.

From the commencement of the 17th to the middle of the 18th century considerable advance was made in the art of music generally. Scarcely a chord, indeed, exists at the present day which is not to be found in the works of J. S. Bach (1685-1750), and G. F. Handel (1685-1759). To Bach is due the consummation of the contrapuntal style of composition.

About the year 1750, and in a great measure due to the influence of Bach, equal temperament gradually came into use, faking the place of the old mean-tone, or unequal system of tuning. The pianoforte (the most important, perhaps, of all musical instruments) now began to become popular; the modern orchestra, also, was established about this time, while the Sonata and Symphony (the highest types of musical composition) were brought to perfection at the hands of Haydn (1732-1809), Mozart (1756-1791), and Beethoven, (1770-1827).

Since the death of Beethoven, who is generally regarded as the greatest musical genius the world has ever seen, no material advance has been made in the science of Harmony. Modern composers are indebted for any originality in their harmonies almost entirely to the employment of discords formed either by the use of auxiliary notes, or by the introduction of the chromatic element. In the matter of harmonic progressions, it is a question whether *any* advance has been made upon the masterpieces of the great composers, or indeed whether any advance can be made, as long as the division of the octave is based upon equal temperament.

The theory of music, it may here be said, comprises the following subjects; the Rudiments of music, Harmony in all its branches, Form in composition, Counterpoint (simple and double), Canon and Fugue, Orchestration, Acoustics as applied to music, a critical knowledge of the greatest musical works, and the general History of the art of music. This course of study will occupy the attention of the average student for a period of at least three years, after which he will begin to learn how little he really knows; for having climbed to the summit of one hill, he will find, rising in all directions, higher and higher still, the summits of other hills—summits which were hidden from view when he was in the vale below. Thus it was with Beethoven, who at the zenith of his career, exclaimed, "I have not studied enough."

The subject of Harmony, for the purposes of study, may be divided into the following branches:—

I.	INTRODUCTORY.	The major and minor diatonic scales, and intervals.
II.	THE COMMON CHORD.	Harmonic progressions, cadences and sequences.
III.	FUNDAMENTAL DISCORDS.	The dominant seventh, modution, secondary sevenths, major and minor ninths and their derivatives.
IV.	SUSPENSIONS.	Single, double and triple, both rising and falling.
V.	AUXILIARY NOTES.	Modified chords, pedals and arpeggios.
VI.	CHROMATIC CHORDS.	Triads, primary sevenths and ninths, and chromatically changed notes.

In addition to the above, wherein the subject is usually treated from the four-part vocal standpoint, the following features, also, will be considered in the present work:—

Harmony for more or less than four voices,

Harmony in its relation to counterpoint, and

Harmony for instruments, especially the string quartet.

It is very important for the student to possess a good general knowledge of all that appertains to the rudiments of music before commencing the study of harmony. A thorough knowledge of the diatonic scales and of intervals being especially important, these subjects will be treated of in the first three chapters. The scales, indeed, are the very alphabet of the language of music; for, just as letters are put together to form words, words to form sentences, and sentences to form a poem, so, in music, notes are put together to form chords, chords to form periods, and periods to form the 'song without words.' In the scale, one note at a time is considered, each note having its own technical name; in the interval, two notes at a time are considered, the effect being either consonant or dissonant; while, in the chord, three or more notes at a time are considered, the combined effect being either a concord or a discord.

Such questions as the value of notes and rests, the meaning of the great stave, the various clefs and their use, the value of the measure (including time and accent), and the significance of the musical terms and signs in ordinary use, belong to the subject of rudiments, and it would be out of place to treat of them in the present work. Let the student not fail to have a perfect mastery over all these matters before commencing to study chapter IV; for, sooner or later, he will learn that the harmonic structure which he is about to erect requires, like architectural structure, a firm and solid foundation.

Furthermore, it is most desirable that the student should possess some knowledge of piano-forte playing and sight-singing; if, indeed, it only is sufficient to sing the melodies, and to play the progressions, contained in his exercises; for an intelligent appreciation of everything he writes is indispensable. He should also learn that music may be appreciated through the medium of the eye, as well as through that of the ear. This faculty of reading music with the understanding, as one would read a book, is not a property appertaining to genius alone; it is rather a property appertaining to talent, and talent is the reward of perseverance and an aptitude for work. In order to acquire this faculty, let the student, in the first place, try to imagine the effect of each progression, and here the sight-singing will be found invaluable, and in the second place, let him test the accuracy of his conclusions, and this may be done by means of the piano. If this plan be conscientiously adopted, he will, in due course, be able to *see* the effect of a passage without singing over the parts, and without making use of the piano at all; for, in the imagination, every chord may be played, every melody sung, and the full intent of every progression perceived and appreciated.

The student, moreover, is strongly advised, in working exercises, to give to each chord as it occurs its proper technical name, and to write under the bass-note the symbol employed to represent the chord. It is not sufficient to call a chord by its alphabetical name alone. The common chord of C, for example, in the key of C, differs altogether in effect from the common chord of C in the key of F (major or minor), and from the same chord in the key of G, or in the key of E minor; but the alphabetical name is the same in all these cases. The character of a chord depends entirely upon the key in which it occurs. Now, by the employment of technical names, for which symbols may if preferred be substituted, the apparently complicated functions of chords are reduced to a remarkable degree of simplicity, as there is but one set of technical names and these, with certain modifications, serve the purpose for every key, major or minor.

In conclusion, let it be said, and it cannot be too strongly emphasized, that the faculty of 'tonal vision,' if such a term may be employed, or, 'hearing with the eye,' as it is frequently called, must in any case and at all costs be acquired before the student can entertain the hope of ultimate success in the realm of Harmony.

CHAPTER I.

THE MAJOR DIATONIC SCALE.

1. A musical sound is the result of *regular vibrations* in the air; irregular vibrations result in what is commonly called noise. Every musical sound possesses three characteristics:

Pitch, the acuteness or gravity of the sound;

Force, its degree of loudness; and

Quality, which depends upon the source of the sound.

The sound known as 'middle C' is regarded as the *standard of pitch in music.*

It is called *middle* C on account of the central position which the note, employed to represent this sound, occupies in the great stave.

Middle C, may be said to be the starting point in the study of Harmony.

The *difference in pitch* between two musical sounds is called an interval. Intervals are measured by **semi-tones ;** a semi-tone, *i.e.*, a half-tone, being the *smallest* difference between any two sounds in music. A semi-tone is therefore known as *the unit of measurement.*

2. A succession of sounds ascending (or descending) regularly is called a **scale** (Lat. *scala*, a ladder). There are two kinds of scales used in music, the **Diatonic** (Gr. *dia*, through, and *tonos*, a tone or sound), and the **Chromatic** (Gr. *chroma*, **colour)**

The construction of the chromatic scale, which consists of semi-tones only, will be considered in a later chapter.

Of the diatonic scale, in which both tones and semi-tones occur, there are two kinds—the Major and the Minor.

The minor scale will be considered in chapter III, a knowledge of intervals being necessary in order to understand its construction.

Another kind of scale known as the Enharmonic should also be mentioned; it can be played on instruments of the violin character, and can also be sung by the voice. In this scale, the sounds are *closer together* than a semi-tone; it is, therefore, *not used in* Harmony. The term enharmonic, at the present day, is exclusively used for a *change in the name of a note*, such as C sharp to D flat, there being *no* change of pitch whatever.

The term key is employed to represent the notes of a diatonic scale taken collectively. This term, however, has really a wider significance, for it comprises also certain chromatic notes.

3. A diatonic scale is named after the note on which it commences, and this note is called the key-note. Any sound in music may be taken as a key-note. There are seven different notes, each with a distinctive letter name, in a scale; to these the octave of the key-note is invariably added to complete the effect. Each note or step is also called a degree.

In a major scale the semi-tones occur between *the third and fourth*, and between *the seventh and eighth* degrees; all the other spaces being tones.

Middle C is taken as the key-note for the first scale, which is therefore called the scale of C major, or simply, the scale of C, the word major being understood. It is also called the natural, and sometimes, the normal scale.

The semi-tones occur between E and F, and between B and C. These are known as *diatonic* semi-tones, to distinguish them from the *chromatic* semi-tone, which is expressed by the use of one letter only, as, for instance, C to C sharp.

Musical notation somewhat fails, it will be seen, to indicate the difference between the tones and semi-tones; all the notes in the above scale being apparently equidistant. The construction of a scale may be exactly represented in the form of a ladder.

In the accompanying diagram the rounds of the ladder are of two kinds, the broad lines represent the notes of the major scale, show-ing the position and the relative size of each tone and semi-tone; while the thin dotted lines indicate the notes which exist between the degrees that are a tone apart; if the scale of C is played on the piano, these notes will be the black keys.

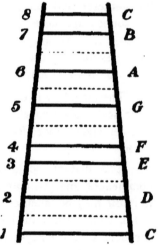

4. A major scale is divisible into two equal parts, of four notes each, called tetrachords (Gr. *tetra*, four, and *chorde*, a string or note). These tetrachords are of *exactly similar construction*, the semi-tones occurring between the third and fourth degrees in each case, the other spaces being tones.

The positions of the semi-tones are indicated by slurs.

In the above example the tetrachords are said to be *dis-junct.* When the last note of one tetrachord becomes the first of the next, the tetrachords are said to be *conjunct*. If a scale is extended for two or more octaves, the successive tetrachords will occur disjunctly and conjunctly, alternately, throughout.

Although any alphabetical group of four notes may be called a tetrachord, yet this term in modern music invariably signifies a tetrachord in which the notes occur in the above order, namely, *tone, tone and semi-tone*.

5. The *principal use* of the tetrachord is in connection with the formation of **new scales.** A new scale may be formed by taking either of the tetrachords in the scale of C, and adding a new tetrachord to it. The new tetrachord will, in every case, necessitate the use of an *accidental*, in order that the semi-tone may occur in the right place; otherwise the scale would still be in the *key* of C.

The *upper* tetrachord in the scale of C may be taken to form the *lower* tetrachord in the scale of G; and in order that the *new upper tetrachord* shall be properly constructed, it will be necessary for the F to be made *sharp*.

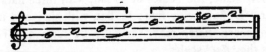

F sharp, now being an integral part of the scale, is placed immediately after the clef signature, and becomes known as the **key signature,** thereby indicating that *every* F in the key is to be sharpened.

The upper tetrachord in the scale of G may next be taken to form the lower tetrachord in the scale of D, and in adding the *new* upper tetrachord the C will now have to be made sharp. The key signature in this case will therefore contain two sharps.

In like manner, by taking the upper tetrachord of each successive new scale, the scales of A, with three sharps; E, with four; B, with five; F sharp, with six; and finally, C sharp, with seven sharps, may severally be formed The above scales, except C (the natural scale), are known as the '*sharp*' scales.

6. The *lower* tetrachord in the scale of C may be taken to form the *upper* tetrachord in the scale of F; and in order that the *new lower tetrachord* shall be properly constructed, it will be necessary for the B to be made *flat*.

B flat, now being an integral part of the scale, is placed in the signature.

The lower tetrachord in the scale of F may next be taken to form the upper tetrachord in the scale of B flat, and in adding the *new* lower tetrachord the E will now have to be made flat. The key signature will therefore contain two flats.

In like manner by taking the lower tetrachord of each successive new scale, the scales of E flat, with three flats; A flat, with four; D flat, with five; G flat, with six; and finally, C flat, with seven flats, may severally be formed. These are known as the '*flat*' scales.

7. The following tables show the signatures of all the sharp and flat keys:—

It will be seen that the *relative positions* of the sharps and flats are invariably the same in both the treble and bass staves. This accounts for the upper G having been chosen as the third sharp in the treble for the key of A; also for the lower F as the last flat in the key of C flat.

The signatures of C sharp and C flat, *especially*, should be committed to memory, for they respectively contain the signatures of *all* the other sharp and flat scales. The signature of the key of E, for example, will be seen if the last three sharps are taken away from the signature of C sharp; and the signature of E flat will be seen if the last four flats are taken away from the signature of C flat.

These signatures, C sharp and C flat, when employed for the alto and tenor clefs, are written as follows:

Alto.

Tenor.

The key of C sharp is rarely employed in music, its place being taken by the key of D flat (with five flats), which is identically the same key. The same may also be said of the key of C flat, which is identically the same as the key of B (with five sharps). When two scales are the same in pitch, but different in name, they are said to be 'enharmonic equivalents.'

8. The tetrachordal system of scale construction may (if desired) be continued *beyond* the scales of C sharp and C flat. The next scale after C sharp would be G sharp, with eight sharps, (one double and six single sharps); after which would come D sharp, with nine sharps; and then A sharp, with ten; and *finally* E sharp, with eleven; for the next scale, B sharp, is *identically the same as the scale of C.* In like manner the flat scales might be continued as far as A double flat; the next scale, D double flat, being *also* identically the same as the scale of C.

The following diagram illustrates the cyclical system upon which the scales are constructed.

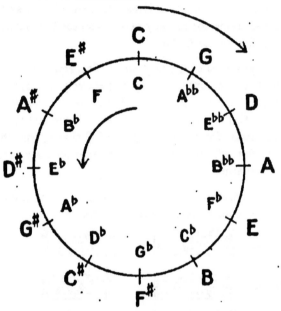

In the above diagram, the sharp scales are on the outer side, and the flat scales on the inner side, of the circle.

By means of the tetrachords a close degree of *relationship* may be said to exist between any given scale and the scales which immediately *precede* and *follow* it; these scales are, therefore, said to be related to the given scale, and are called *attendant* scales.

The scale of C is called the first scale, simply because it is the first to be considered; for in the theory of scale construction there is *no* first scale, any more than there is a beginning to a circle.

9. Each degree of the scale has a technical name, by the use of which *reference* may be made to the functions of any given note, irrespective of its alphabetical name, and regardless

of the pitch of the key. For convenience in writing, these technical names may be represented by *symbols*. The technical names for the degrees of the typical scale of C, together with their symbols, are given in the following table, which should be read upwards.

DEGREE.	SCALE OF C.	TECHNICAL NAME.	SYMBOL.
7th.	B	Leading-note.	L
6th.	A	Submediant.	VI
5th.	G	Dominant.	V
4th.	F	Subdominant.	IV
3rd.	E	Mediant.	III
2nd.	D	Supertonic.	II
1st.	C	Tonic.	I

The Tonic (Lat. *tonus*, sound; Gr. *tonos*, strength) is the tone-note of the key.

Supertonic implies the note *above* the tonic.

The Mediant (Lat. *medium*, middle) is the note midway between the tonic and the dominant, the two most important notes of the key.

Subdominant naturally implies the note below the dominant, but a deeper meaning is possible, namely, that it is the under-dominant, or the fifth below the tonic, and therefore the key-note of the preceding scale.

The Dominant (Lat. *dominus*, lord or ruler) is the note next in importance to the tonic, this is due to its position as the first note of the upper tetrachord, and therefore the key-note of the succeeding scale.

Submediant signifies the third below the tonic, just as the mediant is the third above; or it may be regarded as the note midway between the tonic and the subdominant.

ie Leading-note (A. Sax. *laedan*, to lead or go) is so termed from the strong tendency of this note to rise to the tonic. In French it is appropriately known as *La note sensible*, the sensitive note. The symbol L is employed for this note, instead of VlI, as might have been expected, because, in the first place, it is easier to write ; and, in the second place, because a distinctive symbol more readily directs attention to the characteristics of this note, which, (it may here be said,) not only has, as a rule, a fixed progression, but which, unlike the other notes of the major scale, is never the root of a diatonic common chord, and never the tonic of an attendant key.

SUMMARY.

§ 1. The characteristics of a musical sound.
   Middle C the standard of pitch.   Definition of semitone.

§ 2. Scales in general.
   Diatonic (major and minor), Chromatic and Enharmonic.

§ 3. The scale of C major
   Degrees of the scale represented in the form of a ladder.

§ 4. The tetrachord.
   Order of the notes—tone, tone and semitone.

§ 5. The upper tetrachord.
   The scale of G, and all the sharp scales.

§ 6. The lower tetrachord.
   The scale of F, and all the flat scales.

§ 7. Key signatures.
   The signatures of C sharp and C flat contain the signatures
   of all keys.

§ 8. The cycle keys,
   Illustrative diagram.   Attendant scales.

§ 9. Technical names.
   The symbol for each.   Their derivation and significance.

EXERCISES.

1. State the characteristics of a musical sound.

2. Define and compare the terms, Diatonic, Chromatic, and Enharmonic, as employed in connection with the scales.

3. Explain the use of the tetrachord, and show that any major scale may be formed by tetrachordal construction from its attendant scales.

4. Write the major scales, the signatures of which are:

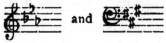 and

5. Write on the treble stave, the scale of E Major; and on the bass stave the scale of A flat major; and mark, with a slur, the position of the semi-tones in each.

6. Give the meaning of the terms, Tonic, Mediant, Dominant and Leading-note; and state why the Submediant is so called.

7. Give the technical name of the note A, when it occurs in the keys of G, B flat, E, D flat, F sharp and C flat.

8. Name the tonic of the scale of which the dominant is:

then write this scale, and write also the enharmonic equivalent of this scale; and in each case mark, with a slur, the tetrachords.

9. By the employment of sharps and flats where necessary, convert the following passages into major scales, the first note in each case to be the tonic.

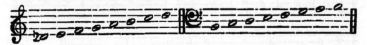

10. Correct the following key signatures :—

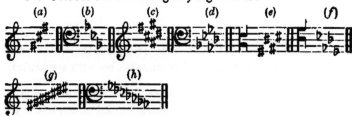

11. Write the key signatures of the scales of which the key-notes are :

 and

12. Name the scales in which the following intervals occur:

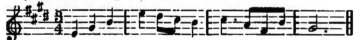

13. Name (a) the subdominant and (b) the leading-note in the keys of D, B flat, E, A flat, F sharp and G flat.

14. Write over each of the notes in the following passage the symbol indicating its technical name.

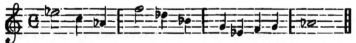

15. Name the key in which the following passage is written, and re-write it, omitting the flats and employing the correct key signature; also insert the symbols.

16. Add the necessary clefs and accidentals (but no key signature) to convert the following melody into (a) the key of B, and (b) the key of D flat.

CHAPTER II.

10. The terms major (greater) and minor (less), as applied to the diatonic scales, require some explanation, for it must not be supposed that by their use it is intended to imply that one scale is greater than another. These terms refer to the interval which exists between the key-note and the third degree, or, to use the technical names, the tonic and the mediant of the scale. In former times the scale of A minor, for example, was known as 'the scale of A with the lesser third,' a designation more definite, perhaps, but certainly less convenient than that which obtains at the present day. Some knowledge of intervals is therefore necessary before the construction of the minor scale can be thoroughly understood.

By an interval is understood *the difference in pitch* between two musical sounds.

11. Intervals, like the lines of the stave and, as will be seen later, the notes of a chord, are always reckoned *upwards* unless the contrary is expressly stated.

An interval is measured by *the number of semi-tones* which it contains.

Every interval has both a *particular* and a *general* name; the latter being an ordinal number, signifying the number of degrees, or letters, concerned; the former being a qualifying name, dependent upon the number of semi-tones concerned.

The unison (Lat. *unus sonus*, one sound,) or prime, though not actually an interval is considered as such for convenience in classification.

The intervals which exist between the tonic of a major scale, as the lower sound, and any degree in that scale, as the upper, are termed **Normal.** The normal intervals in the scale of C, with their respective names, and the number of semi-tones contained in each, are as follows:

This example should be committed to memory; it will be found valuable as the basis for the calculation of all intervals.

The term major implies that a minor interval of the same order exists. A minor interval is always a *semi-tone less* than a major   The term perfect will be explained, and its use justified, in due course. The term *octave* signifies, and is invariably used instead of its numerical equivalent, an eighth.

An interval is said to be **diatonic** when both notes form part of any major diatonic scale; when otherwise, the interval is said to be **chromatic.**

Intervals less than, and including, an octave are termed **simple**; greater than an octave, **compound.**

12. A major scale, *two octaves in extent,* contains *every* simple diatonic interval in that key.

All the seconds, thirds, sixths and sevenths, in the above passage are either *major or minor.* The name of any given interval may be discovered, first by determining the number of

letters concerned, and then either by counting the number of
semi-tones it contains, which is generally best for smaller intervals, or applying, what may be termed, the ' normal test,' which
is certainly best for the larger intervals. For example, the
interval E to G is a *minor third*; for since there are three letters
concerned, viz., E, F and G, it is a *third*; and since the interval contains three semi-tones, it is *minor*. Or, to apply the
normal test, if E is regarded as a tonic, the key will be E with
four sharps, and since the normal or major third is G sharp, E
to G natural, being a semi-tone less, will be minor. The interval F to D is a *major sixth*, for there are six letters concerned,
and F to D is *normal* in the key of F. The interval B to A is
a *minor seventh*, for, in the key of B (with five sharps) the
normal (or major) seventh is A sharp.

All the fourths in the above example are normal in their
respective keys, and therefore *perfect* in the key of C, except
alone F to B, which, being a semi-tone *greater* than perfect, is
said to be *augmented*; likewise all the fifths are *perfect*, except
B to F, which, being a semi-tone *less* than perfect, is said to be
diminished.

The augmented fourth, which occurs only upon the subdominant of
the key, was formerly known as, and is still often called, the Tritone,
(Lat. *Tritonus*, three-toned). It has also been called the *Extreme*, *Sharp*,
Superfluous, and *Pluperfect* fourth. The diminished fifth has also been
cal ed the *False*, *Flat*, and *Imperfect* fifth. The above names, however,
are by no means in ordinary use; in fact, they are rapidly becoming
altogether obsolete.

13. By employing the signs, + for major, − for minor,
× for augmented, and o for diminished, the *names* of intervals
may, for convenience in writing, be represented by symbols.
Thus, for example:

    2 + indicates a major second;
    3 −   "   a minor third;
    4 ×   "   an augmented fourth;
    5 o   "   a diminished fifth.

The sign + may be regarded as representing normal intervals generally, so that when employed in conjunction with either 4 or 5, it would indicate a perfect interval. This sign may often be omitted altogether, being taken for granted, especially when referring to perfect intervals; just as the scale of C major is often called the scale of C, the term major being understood.

14. The following table comprises all the simple diatonic intervals; showing also the symbol employed for each interval, the number of semi-tones contained in each interval, and the frequency of occurrence of each interval in any major scale.

| NAME. | | SYMBOL. | NUMBER OF SEMI-TONES. | FREQUENCY OF OCCURRENCE. |
GENERAL.	PARTICULAR.			
Unison,	Perfect.	1	0	Seven times.
Second,	Minor.	2 –	1	Twice.
	Major.	2 +	2	Five times.
Third,	Minor.	3 –	3	Four times.
	Major.	3 +	4	Three times.
Fourth,	Perfect.	4	5	Six times.
	Augmented.	4 ×	6	Once.
Fifth,	Diminished.	5 o	6	Once.
	Perfect.	5	7	Six times.
Sixth,	Minor.	6 –	8	Three times.
	Major.	6 +	9	Four times.
Seventh,	Minor.	7 –	10	Five times.
	Major.	7 +	11	Twice.
Octave,	Perfect.	8	12	Seven times.

The student should commit to memory the number of semi-tones contained in each of the above intervals; but the major and minor second, the major and minor third, and the perfect fourth should especially be remembered, as the larger intervals (should they be forgotten) may readily be calculated from these.

INTERVALS.

The simple diatonic intervals in the key of C, the octa
nd unison) excepted, together with their symbols, are
llows:

The above example will enable the student to gauge his ability
ming any intervals taken at random from the Ex. in § 12.

15. Since the difference between major and minor inte
ls is a semi-tone, it follows that a major may be convert
to a minor interval, either by lowering the upper note, or l
ising the lower note, a *chromatic semi-tone*; and conversely,
inor may be changed to a major interval. Thus the maj

third at *a*, may be reduced in size a chromatic semi-tone, either as at *b*, or as at *c*. Care must be taken, in such cases, *never* to change the letter name of either note of the interval, for although the intervals at *d* and at *e*, are respectively the same on the piano as those at *b* and at *c*, yet not only do they differ in *name* (being seconds) but, as will be duly explained, they differ also in *effect*.

The diatonic intervals above the given note C are as follows :—

16. Theoretically speaking, all the major and perfect intervals may be *augmented*, by being increased a chromatic semitone; and all the minor and perfect intervals may be *diminished*, by being decreased a chromatic semi-tone. Practically speaking, however, some of these intervals, notably the augmented third and the diminished sixth, contain exactly the same number of semi-tones as a perfect interval, and for this reason are *not used in harmony.* * Intervals so derived are almost invariably chromatic; the augmented fourth and the diminished fifth, however, are *ambiguous*, for they are sometimes chromatic, and, as has already been seen, sometimes diatonic.

* Although some of these very intervals have occasionally been introduced into modern compositions by the employment of chromatic auxiliary notes, yet nevertheless they do not exist between the notes of any of the accepted chords in harmony.

The chromatic intervals above the given note C are as follows :—

The following example comprises all the simple intervals, both diatonic and chromatic, as employed in harmony above the given note C.

17. Compound intervals have the same qualifying terms as their corresponding simple forms. Thus, the interval at *a* is a *major ninth*, or a compound major second; at *b*, it is a *minor tenth*; at *c* it is a *perfect eleventh*. With the exception of the ninth, however, compound intervals are almost invariably regarded as though they were simple intervals; the interval at *b*, being called a minor third, and that at *c*, a perfect fourth.

18. An interval is said to be **inverted** when the lower sound is placed *above* the upper, or vice versa. Perfect intervals when inverted *remain* perfect; major intervals *change* to minor, and minor to major; augmented intervals *change* to diminished, and diminished to augmented. The numerical name of an inverted interval may be found by subtracting the numerical name of the (uninverted) interval from the number *nine* Thus, the inversions of the normal intervals in § 11 will be as follows :—

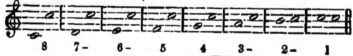

19. An interval is said to be **melodic** when the two sounds are heard in *succession*, and **harmonic** when they are heard in *combination*.

Harmonic intervals are divided into two classes, namely, **consonant**, when the effect is pleasant, and **dissonant**, when otherwise.

The consonant intervals are sub-divided into two classes, namely, *perfect* and *imperfect*; the perfect consonant intervals comprising the fourth, the fifth and the octave, including also the unison; the imperfect, comprising the major and minor thirds and the major and minor sixths.

The dissonant intervals are also sub-divided into two classes, namely, *diatonic* and *chromatic*; the diatonic comprising the major and minor seconds and sevenths, the augmented fourth and the diminished fifth.

The perfect fourth though *rightly* classed as a consonant interval, has, nevertheless, a *dissonant effect* under certain conditions. This question will be considered in due course; in the meantime, it may be said that the dissonant effect arises when this interval exists between the bass and any of the upper notes of a chord.

INTERVALS

WITH REFERENCE TO THEIR MUSICAL EFFECT.

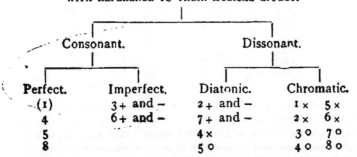

Consonant.		Dissonant.	
Perfect.	Imperfect.	Diatonic.	Chromatic.
(1)	3+ and −	2+ and −	1× 5×
4	6+ and −	7+ and −	2× 6×
5		4×	3○ 7○
8		5○	4○ 8○

The consonant intervals are naturally all diatonic, but at the same time it may be said that all the diatonic intervals occasionally possess a chromatic character. For example, should the note F sharp occur in the key of C, it would form a chromatic interval with each of the diatonic notes in this key, and such intervals would be termed chromatic, notwithstanding that they are diatonic in the key of G.

20. Fourths and fifths are called *perfect*, it may now be said, because, in the first place these intervals are practically in tune with the natural fourth and fifth, which cannot be said of the imperfect consonant intervals*; secondly, because when

---

* This point will be explained in a later chapter, when the subject of Acoustics, in relation to Harmony is under consideration. Reference to these natural intervals will be found in § 34 Chap. IV.

inverted they remain perfect; and thirdly, because intervals consisting of five and seven semi-tones, respectively, are not recognized in harmony under any other name than perfect. Each of the imperfect consonant intervals may be *enharmonically* changed into a dissonant interval. For example, the interval C to A flat, *a minor sixth*, is exactly the same in size, eight semi-tones, (and therefore exactly the same on the piano,) as C to G sharp, an *augmented fifth*. These intervals, moreover, have not only different names, but they have also equally different effects, which, if the following passage is played on the piano, will be readily appreciated :—

The common chords in the above example are employed in order to establish the keys in which these two intervals are respectively found ; for, of course, there would be no difference if they were played in immediate succession, and irrespective of any key relationship whatever. To obtain a clear idea of this matter, the student must possess some knowledge of the minor scale, and of the major and minor common chords.

Doubly augmented, and doubly diminished intervals, such as

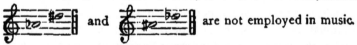 and are not employed in music.

It is of primary importance that the student should be able not only to *name* a given interval, but that he should also be able to recognize its effect, before commencing the study of harmony. With a little practice and perseverance he will learn to appreciate the effect as quickly with the *eye* as with the *ear*, and not indeed till this is accomplished can he hope to acquire that indispensable faculty of 'tonal-vision' to which reference was made in the introductory chapter.

SUMMARY.

§ 10. The terms 'major' and 'minor' as appl'ed to scales.

An interval—the difference in pitch between two sounds.

§ 11. The Normal intervals.

Intervals are reckoned upwards; are measured by semi-tones; have both a particular and general name; may be diatonic or chromatic; simple or compound; melo-dic or harmonic; consonant or dissonant.

§ 12. The simple diatonic intervals.

The 'normal test.'

§ 13. The symbols.

+ major, – minor, × augmented, o diminished.

§ 14. Diatonic intervals tabulated.

Example, with each interval named.

§ 15. Diatonic intervals above a given note.

Chromatic and alphabetical changes.

§ 16. Chromatic intervals.

2o, 3×, 6o and 7×, not used in music, being by enhar-monic changes the same as perfect intervals.

§ 17. Compound intervals.

Usually regarded as simple, except the ninth.

§ 18. The inversion of intervals.

Subtract the numerical name from the number 9; change + to –, – to +, × to o, and o to ×; perfect remains perfect.

§ 19. Intervals with reference to their musical effect.

Table classifying the consonant and dissonant intervals. Melodic and Harmonic intervals.

§ 20. Enharmonically changed intervals.

Perfect intervals alone not thus changed.

The same two sounds may differ not only in name but also in effect.

Ability to recognize the effect of an interval (tonal-vision) a necessity in the study of Harmony.

EXERCISES.

1. Explain the significance of the terms 'major' and 'minor' as applied to the diatonic scales.

2. Name the following intervals.

3. Write and name the inversions of each of the above intervals.

4. Name the following intervals, and give the number of semitones contained in each.

5. State the effect, consonant or dissonant, of each of the above intervals.

6. Explain the difference between a diatonic and a chromatic semitone, and give an example of each above the notes F sharp and A flat.

7. Distinguish between two sounds heard in succession and in combination.

8. Write examples of the following intervals both above and below the note B (third line in the treble): major second, minor third, augmented fourth, diminished fifth, major seventh and minor ninth.

9. Name the note, giving also its technical name (it occurs in one major scale only), upon which it is impossible to form the interval of an augmented fifth. Mention any other impracticable intervals.

10. Write and name the normal intervals in the scales of B major and D flat major.

11. Name the interval between the upper tonic of a scale and each degree *below*; as for example, the tonic *down* to the leading-note, the tonic *down* to the submediant, and so on.

12. Give examples of the following intervals in the keys of A major and E flat major; in no case employing the tonic.

2-, 3+, 4×, 5 ο, 6-, 7+.

13. Show that all the consonant intervals are contained in each of the following arpeggios.

14. Complete the following chromatic scale, by inserting in the vacant spaces the intervals named below, calculating each interval from the note C.

1× 2× 4× 5× 6× 7- 6- 5ο 3- 2-

15. Write above the note E, (*a*) all the diatonic intervals, and (*b*) all the chromatic intervals used in music.

16. Change the following intervals chromatically, as many times as possible, without the use of double sharps or double flats, and give the name and the effect (consonant or dissonant) in each case.

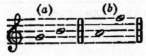

17. Change the upper note of the above intervals (Question 16) enharmonically, and re-name them accordingly.

18. Name all the major scales in which each of the following intervals occur.

19. Compare the following pairs of intervals as to their effect upon the ear, and state why the first interval in each case is diatonic and consonant while the second is chromatic and dissonant.

20. Name the following intervals, give the number of semitones contained in each, state the effect, and write the inversion of each interval.

It is suggested that the above exercise be worked in tabular form, thus:—

INTERVAL.	NAME.	SEMI-TONES.	EFFECT.	INVERSION.
(e)	3 ○	2	Dis.	6 ×

The above exercise, for the purpose of practice, may also be worked with the bass clef employed instead of the treble.

CHAPTER III.

21. The difference between the major and the minor diatonic scales is due to the difference in effect between the major and minor imperfect consonant intervals. These intervals which occur between the tonic and the mediant, and between the tonic and the submediant, are both major in the major scale, while in the minor scale, the *true* minor scale, they are both minor. The supertonic, subdominant, dominant and leading note are at exactly the same intervals above the tonic in both scales.

The term *mode*, signifying method or manner, is frequently employed instead of the word 'scale,' when reference is made to the difference in character between the major and minor scales.

Unlike the major scale, which never varies in its formation, the minor scale exists in a variety of forms. One of these *alone*, that alluded to above as the true minor scale, is employed in harmony, and hence it is called the harmonic minor scale. All other forms may be regarded as modifications of this scale.

The normal form of the minor scale, sometimes called the *ancient* or *historic* minor, is as follows:—

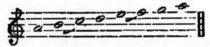

The slurs in the above and in the following examples indicate the positions of the semi-tones.

22. In the above scale, which is now practically obsolete, the intervals between the tonic and the mediant, and between the tonic and submediant are, it will be seen, respectively, a minor third and a minor sixth; there is, however, *no* leading-note, the seventh and eighth degrees being a tone apart. In order to obtain a leading-note, this note being equally as important in the minor key as in the major, the subtonic (as the minor seventh of the tonic is called) must be *chromatically raised a semi-tone ;* the scale then becomes the *true,* or the *harmonic* minor scale.

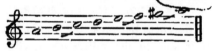

23. The interval between the sixth and seventh degrees in the harmonic minor scale is an *augmented second,* and therefore, being a chromatic interval, is regarded as unmelodious. To avoid this interval, and it should almost invariably be avoided in melodies, the following important modification of the harmonic form, called the *melodic* minor scale, is employed :—

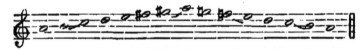

Here, the augmented second is avoided in ascending by chromatically raising the submediant, that is to say, by the employment of the *major* submediant (+VI); while, in descending, in order that the minor submediant may be introduced, the leading note is sacrificed, the *subtonic* (VII) taking its place.

24. The melodic form of the minor scale is by far the most important modification of the true minor scale. This scale has, occasionally, been employed with the descending form the same as the ascending, more especially by the older masters, such as Bach and Handel. This form of the scale, however, has never been in general use, probably on account of the entire absence of the minor submediant.

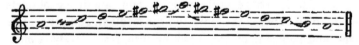

All other modifications of the minor scale arise from the combination of the harmonic and melodic forms; the following, in which the leading-note appears in ascending, and in which the minor submediant is also present, being the most important:—

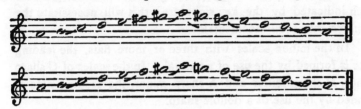

These scales also are by no means in general use, and have, therefore, no specific names.

25. Each major scale has what is termed a relative minor scale, the key-note of which is the submediant of the major; and conversely, each minor scale has a *relative* major, the key-note of which is the mediant of the minor. The relative minor of C major is A minor; and the relative major of A minor is C major.

Relative scales have the *same* key signatures; this necessitates the use of an accidental whenever the leading-note of a minor key is employed.

Each major scale has, also, what is termed a tonic minor, and each minor scale, a tonic major; the key-notes in these cases being the *same* tonic. The tonic minor of C major is C minor, which is the relative minor of E flat.

Minor scales are constructed from major scales, either from the relative or from the tonic major, and not, like the major scales, from one another. The tetrachord, which played such an important part in the construction of the major scales, does not enter at all into the construction of the minor scales.

26. To construct the relative harmonic minor of any given major scale, first write the major key signature, then write a scale commencing on the submediant of the major scale, and add the necessary accidental to raise the seventh degree a chromatic semi-tone. The melodic minor may be formed by

chromatically raising both the sixth and seventh degrees in ascending, and by restoring these degrees in descending to the pitch indicated by the key signature; this will necessitate the employment of *four* accidentals.

In the minor scales with three or more flats, the leading note is formed by the use of a natural. In the scales of G sharp minor, D sharp minor and A sharp minor, the leading-note is formed by the use of a double sharp.

The following diagram exhibits all the major scales with their relative minors. The larger capitals indicate the tonics of the major keys; the smaller, the tonics of the minor. The numerals indicate the number of sharps or flats in the signature.

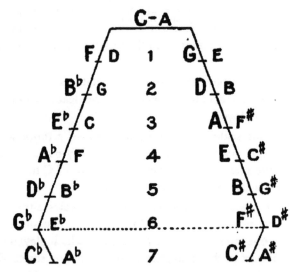

27 On account of the key signature being the same for both a major scale and its relative minor, students are apt to find some difficulty in determining the key in which a musical composition is written. The following example illustrates the relationship between the keys of C major and A minor. Here, it will be seen that all the notes in the scale of C occur also in

the scale of A minor, except the dominant (V) which is chromatically raised to form the leading-note (L) in the scale of A minor.

If, therefore, the dominant of the major key, indicated by the signature, is found in the first two or three measures of a composition, the key will be that major key; if, however, this note is found accidentally changed in the first two or three measures, the composition will be in the minor key; while, it may here be added, the last note in the bass in every composition is *invariably* the tonic of the key.

28. The harmonic form of the tonic minor scale may be constructed by chromatically lowering the *mediant* and *sub-mediant* of the major scale. Thus, the harmonic form of C minor is as a follows :—

This scale should, however, be written thus·—

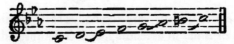

The melodic form of C minor is as follows:—

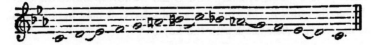

29. The notes employed in the construction of the scales of C major and C minor (melodic form) constitute almost a chromatic scale. If to these the *minor second* of the tonic is added, so that the seconds, thirds, sixths and sevenths appear in both their major and minor forms; and if to these the *augmented fourth* of the tonic is added, the augmented fourth being more closely related to the tonic than is the diminished fifth, the chromatic scale will be *complete*. This scale, now generally known as **the harmonic form of the chromatic scale,** is as follows:—

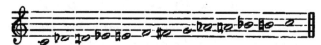

A scale of similar construction may be formed from any major key-note, but it is *imperative* that the intervals throughout be the same as in the above example, whether the scale is employed in its ascending or descending form.

30. The chromatic scale of C is, however, more usually written as in the following example, when, for the sake of distinction, it is termed **the melodic form of the chromatic scale.**

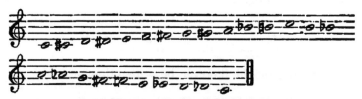

Composers frequently vary the above scale by employing A sharp instead of B flat in ascending, and G flat instead of F sharp in descending, in order to reduce the number of requisite accidentals; these notes, A sharp and G flat however, unlike the other chromatic notes in the above example, have, it may here be said, *no harmonic relationship* with the key of C.

31. Finally, when all the notes employed in the melodic form of the chromatic scale of C are placed in gradual ascending order, an enharmonic scale will be formed, a scale which *alone* meets the requirements of the modern composer, and which may therefore be termed the modern enharmonic scale of C.

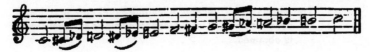

The half notes in the above example are the diatonic notes of the scale; the quarter-notes are the *perfect* chromatics, and being diatonic to the attendant major keys (see § 8), they are never enharmonically changed; the eighth notes are the *imperfect* chromatics, and may be employed in either form.

To the above scale, as the basis of modern harmony, the author attaches the greatest importance (see also the Preface, page xi). As a scale however, it will not enter very deeply into the work of the student for the present. The only notes in this scale, besides the half-notes, which have generally accepted technical names are the D flat, E flat and A flat, these are known respectively as the minor supertonic (– II), the minor mediant (– III) and the minor submediant (– VI). In Appendix I, technical names are suggested for the other notes of this scale.

The harmonic basis of this scale will be explained in a later chapter, when the chromatic element in Harmony is under consideration. For the present, the attention of the student should be confined to the construction of the diatonic scales, both individually, and in relation to one another, the ability to recognize at sight the key in which a composition is written being most important; for key relationship is the basis of modulation, while modulation, which is the art of changing from one key to another, is, in conjunction with Harmony, the basis of all musical composition.

SUMMARY.

§ 21. The Normal form of the minor scale.

The mediant, and the submediant, especially the former, are the characteristic degrees of the diatonic scales.

§ 22. The Harmonic form of the minor scale.

The normal form, lacking a leading-note, now practically obsolete; with L introduced, the true or harmonic form is obtained.

§ 23. The Melodic form of the minor scale.

Employed in order to avoid the unmelodious 2×️ of the harmonic form.

§ 24. Various modified forms of the minor scale.

Three examples (with no specific names) in occasional use.

§ 25. The Relative minor scale.

It commences on VI of the major scale, and has the same key signature as the major scale.

§ 26. Diagram of major and relative minor scales.

This should be committed to memory.

§ 27. Two rules for determining the mode.

L of the minor mode requires an accidental; the last bass-note invariably the tonic.

§ 28. The Tonic minor scale.

The harmonic and melodic forms of C minor.

§ 29. The Harmonic form of the Chromatic scale.

The chromatic notes are formed by the intervals, 2-, 3-, 4×, 6- and 7-, calculated from the tonic.

§ 30. The Melodic form of the Chromatic scale.

In ascending 1×, 2× and 5× are employed; in descending, and in other respects, this scale resembles the harmonic form.

§ 31. The Modern Enharmonic scale.

The basis of the chromatic element in harmony.

EXERCISES.

1. Explain the chief points of difference between the major and the minor scales.

2. Write the minor scales, in both their harmonic and melodic forms, the signatures of which are:

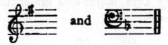

and

3. Write the relative minor of B flat in its harmonic form; and the tonic minor of B in its melodic form; each ascending and descending, on both the treble and bass staves.

4. Write the scale of F sharp minor in its *true* form, and then re-write the same exemplifying the modifications of the minor scale in general and in occasional use.

5. Name the leading-note in each of the following minor scales: C sharp, F, B, G, D sharp and E flat.

6. Name the minor scales (one in each case) in which the following intervals occur.

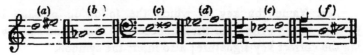

7. Add the accidentals necessary to convert the following passages into harmonic minor scales.

8. Name the minor scales in which the note A is respectively, III, V, L, VI, IV and II.

9. Write, employing the signature of C sharp major, the scale of C sharp minor; and state the relationship which exists between these two scales.

10. Name the minor scales (three in each case) in which the following intervals occur.

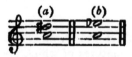

11. State the keys, major and minor, of which the signatures are as follows:

12. Name the relative minors of the major scales, the tonic minors of which are G sharp and D sharp.

13. Write over each of the notes in the following passage the symbol indicating its technical name.

14. Name the key in which the following passage is written, and re-write it omitting unnecessary sharps and employing the correct key signature; also insert the symbols.

15. Write, on the treble-stave, the harmonic form of the chromatic scale of E flat; and on the bass stave, the melodic form of the chromatic scale of A; both ascending and descending.

16. Show that the modern enharmonic scale of C (§ 31) contains all the leading-notes in the attendant keys of C, namely, G major, F major, A minor, E minor and D minor.

CHAPTER IV.

THE COMMON CHORD.

32. Harmony is the science which treats of chords.
A chord is the combination of three or more musical sounds, varying in pitch and occurring simultaneously.

When the interval between any two notes of a chord is *consonant*, the chord is called a **concord ;** when one or more of the intervals are *dissonant*, it is called a **discord.**

Chords are formed in the first instance by adding thirds successively above a given note; this note is called the *root* of the chord.

Middle C, *a*, may be said to be the starting point in the study of Harmony. When one third is added to this note, as at *b*, the result, (as has already been seen) is an interval; when another third is added, as at *c*, the result is a *chord*.

If another third were added to the chord at *c*, the result would be a chord of the *seventh*; and the addition of yet another third would result in a chord of the *ninth*. The chord at *c* is a concord, chords of the seventh and ninth are discords.

A chord consisting of three notes only, or in other words, a note with its third and fifth only, is called a **triad.**

The term 'note' has a double significance in music ; it is employed not only to indicate the written character representing a musical sound, but also to indicate some particular sound itself. The term 'tone,' likewise, has a double significance ; it is employed not only to indicate a musical sound, but also to indicate an interval consisting of two semitones. In Acoustics there are major and minor tones, see also Preface, page x.

By the use of major and minor thirds, which alone are employed in chord construction, *four different kinds of triads* are obtained; these with their symbols and constituent intervals are shown in the following table:

NAME.	SYMBOL.	CONSTRUCTION.
Major.	+	3+ and 3-
Minor.	−	3- and 3+
Augmented.	×	3+ and 3+
Diminished.	o	3- and 3-

The major and minor triads are *concords*; the augmented and diminished, *discords*. These triads, formed upon the note C, are illustrated in the following example.

The triads form the basis of all chords used in musical composition. The major and minor triads are indeed the *only* concords possible; hence, a consonant triad is generally known and spoken of as a common chord, major or minor as the case may be, especially when it is employed in connection with other chords.

33. A triad may be formed upon each degree of the major and the (harmonic) minor scales. The following table (which should be read upwards) comprises all the triads with their respective symbols, as they occur in the diatonic scales.

Melodic symbols, it will be seen, indicate notes only, harmonic symbols indicate chords, see Appendix I. The sign 'o' after the symbol 'L,' is frequently omitted, being understood.

THE DEGREES OF THE SCALES.		THE TRIADS WITH THEIR SYMBOLS (HARMONIC).	
TECHNICAL NAMES.	SYMBOLS (MELODIC).	MAJOR.	MINOR.
Leading-note.	L	Lᴏ	Lo
Submediant.	VI	VI –	VI +
Dominant.	V	V +.	V +
Subdominant.	IV	IV +	IV –
Mediant.	III	III –	III ×
Supertonic.	II	II ¬	IIo
Tonic.	I	I +	I –

The above triads as they occur in the keys of C major and C minor are shown in the following example.

C Major.

I+   II –   III –   IV+   V+   VI –   Lo

C Minor.

I–   IIo   III ×   IV–   V+   VI+   Lo

The student would do well to commit to memory the alphabetical names of the above triads, for these are the same in all keys, whatever the character of the triad may be.

The harmonic form of the minor scale will for the present· alone be employed, and it is necessary to remember that L, in the minor mode, invariably requires an accidental. By the use of +VI (the major submediant) and VII (the subtonic), notes borrowed from the melodic form of the minor scale, certain additional triads, occasionally employed in the minor mode, are obtained, but these will be considered in a later chapter.

34. The consonant triads are divided into two classes, primary and secondary. The classification of the triads in both modes is shown in the following example.

Consonant.		Dissonant.	
Primary.	Secondary.	Diminished.	Augmented.
I+ IV+ V+	II- III- VI-	Lo	
I- IV- V+	VI+	IIo Lo	III ×

The primary triads constitute the *harmonic basis* of the diatonic scales, the origin of which may now be explained. Upon the note C, as the standard of pitch in music (§ 1) a major triad is formed (*a*), to this triad two other triads are added, one of which has for its fifth the root of the triad of C, while the other has for its root the fifth of the triad of C. These three triads contain the notes which form the scale of C (*b*), they therefore contain the key signature of C (*c*).

If now each of these triads is converted into a minor triad (*d*), then the normal (or ancient) form of the scale of C minor is obtained (*e*), while the three flats which thus arise constitute the key signature of C minor (*f*). It will thus be seen that this signature is derived without any reference to or connection with the relative major scale.

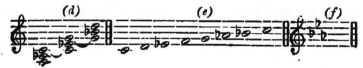

Furthermore, the normal form of the scale of A minor, the relative minor of C, may be obtained by taking the relative minor triads of the above three major triads. The subtonic (VII) must, of course, be chromatically raised in order to form L, when these minor scales are used in harmony.

In a later chapter, the harmonic basis of the chromatic scale will be considered, also the harmonic basis of the modern enharmonic scale (§ 31). The origin of the major triad is to be found in natural science. This triad, the basis of all music, may be easily obtained by performing the following simple experiment. Take an ordinary piece of string, say five feet in length, and mark it off into inches; then stretch it tightly between two points, so that when plucked it will produce a definite musical sound. Supposing this sound were represented by the low C (1)—as a matter of fact it is immaterial what particular sound is produced—then the sound produced when one half of the string (30 inches) is plucked (the other part not being allowed to vibrate) will be the octave above that C (2); when one third of the string (20 inches) is plucked the sound produced will be G (3); one fourth of the string (15 inches) will produce middle C (4); one fifth (12 inches) will produce E (5); and one sixth (10 inches) will produce G (6). The fourth, fifth and sixth divisions of the string, it will be seen, respectively produce the root, third and fifth of the major triad, hence this triad is often called 'the common chord of nature.'

35. It is customary in commencing the study of harmony to arrange chords for the four ordinary voices—Soprano (or Treble), Alto, Tenor and Bass.

The general compass of each of these voices is as follows:

The voices are often termed *parts*, hence the expression,
four-part harmony. Harmony is always understood to be in
four parts, unless some other number of parts is expressly stated.

Since a triad consists of three different notes only, it is
necessary in four-part harmony for one of these notes to be
taken by two different voices. This is called *doubling* the
note. The note doubled may be at the unison or at the distance
of one or more octaves. It is generally best to double the *root*,
which for the present will always be in the bass; when a note
other than the root is in the bass, the chord is said to be
inverted

In arranging the notes of a common chord for voices, any
note in a given chord may, as a matter of fact, be given to
any voice, provided that the note lies within the compass of
that voice, and that certain rules with regard to the relative
position of the parts are observed.

36. A common chord may be arranged for four voices, in
accordance with the following table :

Regular positions.	Close.	When the alto part is at the interval of a third or fourth from its approximate voices (treble and tenor).
	Open.	When the Alto part is at the interval of a fifth or sixth from its approximate voices.
Irregular positions.	Complete.	When the fifth or third is doubled, instead of the root, no note being omitted.
	Incomplete.	When the fifth is omitted; the third must never be omitted.

The regular positions should be employed *as much as
possible*; the irregular positions, however, are very important,
but their use is only justified, as a rule, by their relationship to
the chords which immediately precede and follow them.

In close position, the upper parts are placed as close together as possible; in open position, the parts are distributed as evenly as possible. In no case should the interval of an octave be exceeded between the treble and alto, or between the alto and tenor; the tenor and bass may be a tenth or even a twelfth apart, but not more than a twelfth. Furthermore, the parts should not cross one another, that is to say, the tenor, for example, should not take a higher note than the alto, nor the alto a higher note than the treble. Close position is generally advisable when the treble note is *below* the middle line (B), and open position when it is above this line.

In actual composition many—possibly all—of the rules laid down in harmony are from time to time broken or set aside; this fact, however, in no way lessens the value of rules or justifies their infringement by the student. It has been well said that he alone knows when to break a rule who knows how to keep it.

The following example illustrates the common chord of C arranged for four voices in various ways. At *a, b, c, d* and *e*, the chords are in close position; at *f, g, h* and *i*, they are in open position. At *a* the treble is taking the lowest note of its compass; at *e* the the tenor is taking the highest; and at *i* both treble and alto are taking their highest notes. As a general rule the exreme notes of the compass should be avoided, and indeed it is rarely advisable to let either the alto or the tenor go below their respective positions in the chord at *a*.

Of the above chords, the positions at *b* and *c* for close, and at *g* and *h* for open, may be regarded as being the most desirable. The ‘balance,’ as it is called, of the chord is better in these cases than it is at *e* and *i*, for example.

At *j*, *k* and *l*, the fifth of the chord is doubled; at *m*, *n* and *o*, the third is doubled; and at *p*, *q* and *r*, the chord is in its incomplete form, the fifth being omitted. At *m* and at *p*, the treble and alto are in unison; at *q*, the alto and tenor are in unison. The position of the chord at *j* may be said to be ambiguous, as the treble and alto parts are in close, while the alto and tenor are in open position. Similarly, the chords at *o* and *r* may also be said to be in ambiguous position.

The chords in both of the above examples (*a* to *r*) are all formed from the triad of C major, but they would be equally effective if formed from the triad of C minor; diminished and augmented triads, however, being dissonant, are treated from a different standpoint, and will be considered in a later chapter.

In the following example the chords are all *badly* arranged. At *s*, *t*, *u* and *v*, the interval of an octave is exceeded between the alto and tenor; at *w* and *x*, this interval is exceeded between the treble and alto. At *y* and *z*, the third of the chord is omitted, these chords therefore lack character, being neither definitely major or minor.

37. The subject of harmony is studied principally by means of exercises. These exercises as a rule consist of one given part, to which three other parts are to be added, making in all complete four-part harmony. The given part is usually the bass, and the chords to be employed are indicated by certain *figures*, placed under (or over) the bass notes, these figures representing the intervals between the bass-note and the upper notes of the chord. The figures employed for the common chord are $\frac{5}{3}$, but in the case of the common chord the figures are almost invariably omitted, being understood. The given part may also be the treble, or one of the inner parts.

When a chord, such as V+ in the minor mode, contains a note not in accordance with the key signature, a corresponding accidental is placed under (or over) the bass-note; this accidental, when standing alone, refers to the third of the chord only. When the fifth of the chord is to be thus changed, as in III × of the minor mode, the figure 5, preceded by the necessary accidental, is then placed below the bass. When a chord containing an accidentally-changed note is immediately repeated, it is customary to use the sign ~ under the following bass-note, instead of repeating the accidental; this sign is termed *the line of continuation*.

In writing exercises, it is usual to employ *close score*, the treble and alto parts being written on the treble stave, and the tenor and bass parts on the bass stave, as at *a*. When the notes have stems, the treble and tenor are turned up, and the alto and bass are turned down.

(a)

At *b* and *c*, the above chords are transcribed to *open score*. At *b*, the C clef is used for the alto and tenor parts; this is the form expected from candidates at examinations, when open score is required. At *c*, the method usually adopted by modern com-posers and publishers is exemplified. In open score, the stems of notes *above* the middle line are turned *down* and vice versa; the stems of those *on* the middle line may be turned in either direction.

38. When the given part is in the bass, the upper parts may be arranged in accordance with the principles explained in § 36, the notes of the triad indicated by the bass-note alone being employed.

When the given note is in the treble or an inner part, it is necessary in the first place to determine the roots of the three triads to which it belongs. The root chosen is then placed in the bass, and the position of the chord having been decided upon, the upper parts are added accordingly.

The possible roots for a note when not in the bass are (1) the note itself, (2) the third below, major or minor, according to the key, and (3) the perfect fifth below; major and minor triads for the present alone being employed. The use of the diminished and the augmented triads, and their treatment as discords, will be explained in Chapter VI.

The note C, for example, as a given treble note, may thus be harmonized as the octave in I+, *a*, the third in VI -, *b*, and the fifth in IV +, *c*. Each chord is here shown in both close and open position:

When the given note is in the alto or tenor, the same chords may be employed as if it were in the treble. At *d*, *e* and *f*, middle C is harmonized as an alto note, with the chords in close position ; at *g*, *h* and *i*, middle C is harmonized as a tenor note, with the chords in open position.

Although it is preferable, as a rule (as was stated above) to double the root of a chord, yet the fifth, if desired, may be doubled instead ; the third, however, should rarely be doubled. In the dominant chord, V+, it is an inviolable rule that the third—the leading-note—must never be doubled. On account of its relationship to other chords, it is sometimes necessary to double the third in VI ; this subject of chord relationship, under the heading of Harmonic progressions, will be considered in the succeeding chapter.

SUMMARY.

§ 32. Definition of harmony.

> Concord and discord ; the four kinds of triads.

§ 33. The triads as they occur in the diatonic scales.

> The table of triads, especially the harmonic symbols, should be committed to memory.

§ 34. The classification of the triads.

> The harmonic basis of the diatonic scales.

§ 35. The four voices, or parts.

> The compass of each voice; the root, (for the present) always in the bass, is generally the best note to double.

§ 36. The common chord arranged for voices.

> The regular (close and open) positions, and the irregular (complete and incomplete) positions.

§ 37. The figured bass in exercises.

> The figuring of the common chord ; the significance of an accidental placed below the bass. Close and open score.

§ 38. On working exercises.

> (1) with the given part in the bass, (2) with the given part in the treble, alto or tenor.

EXERCISES.

TRIADS.

1. Define a triad, explain the formation of chords, and state the difference between a concord and a discord.

2. Write an example of each kind of triad upon the notes, G, F, E flat and C sharp.

3. Write and name (or symbolize) all the triads in the keys of (a) D and (b) B flat.

4. Write and name (or symbolize) all the triads in the keys of (a) B minor and (b) G minor.

5. Give the signatures of the keys of which the following are the tonic triads.

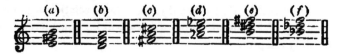

6. Name the keys in which each of the above triads occurs (1) as the subdominant and (2) as the submediant.

7. Name the five keys in which each of the following triads are found, and state when they occur as primary and when as secondary triads.

8. State the character of the following triads, and name the minor keys in which they occur.

9 Write an example of each kind of triad *below* each of the following notes.

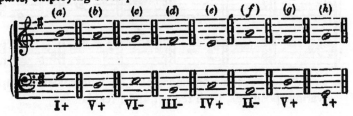

10. Write the triads, V+, IV−, VI+, III×, Lo and IIo, in (a) C sharp minor and (b) F minor.

11. Explain the harmonic basis of the scale of G.

12. Show that the scale of D minor (with its ·correct key signature) may be formed from the scale of D major, without any reference to the scale of F.

THE COMMON CHORD.

I.

13. Add alto and tenor parts to the following treble and bass parts, employing close position.

14. Add alto and tenor parts to the following, employing open position.

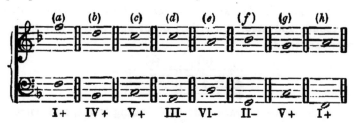

15. Give the compass of each of the four voices, each on its own stave (employing the proper clef for each voice).

16. Explain the various positions in which a common chord may be arranged for voices.

17. Write the common chord of E for four voices, in three different ways, each in close position.

18. Write the common chord of A flat for four voices, in three different ways, each in open position.

Add treble, alto and tenor parts to the following bass-notes; each chord may be worked in two or three different ways.

19. In close position.

20. In open position.

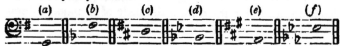

21. Criticise the position of the parts in the following chords.

22. Write the common chord of F for four voices, exemplifying various positions, both regular and irregular.

23. Write for four voices the chord of the dominant (V+) in the keys of C sharp minor, F minor, G sharp minor and B flat minor. Place L in the treble for each chord.*

* When the position is not mentioned, the student may take either close or open, but should not, for the present, take an irregular position.

24. Write the following chords, employing open score :

(a) In the key of E flat.

VI-, III-, IV+, II-, V+ and I+.

(b) In the key of F sharp minor.

VI+, IV-, V+ and I.

II.

Add alto, tenor and bass parts to the following treble notes, harmonizing each note with three different chords.

25. In the key of A.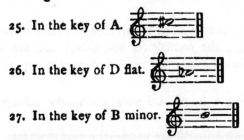

26. In the key of D flat.

27. In the key of B minor.

Add the other voices to the following inner parts ; write in open score. Each note should be harmonized with three different chords, and each chord in both close and open position.

28.  29.

30. Explain the meaning of 'the common chord of nature.'

CHAPTER V.

39. When two common chords (with different roots) follow one another in immediate succession the effect is termed a **harmonic progression.** There are *six* possible harmonic progressions, namely, when the roots rise or fall a second, third or fourth. Roots rising a fifth are the same as falling a fourth, and vice versa. Roots moving a sixth, on account of the large skip, are generally avoided; their effect, however, is practically the same as roots moving a third. Roots moving a seventh are disallowed.

These harmonic progressions are divided into three classes: The *good* (or strong); the *possible* (or tolerable); and the *bad* (or weak), which should rarely be employed except for some particular effect.

(*a*) Roots rising a fourth are very good—the strongest of all.*

(*b*) Roots falling a fourth are good—the next strongest.

(*c*) Roots rising a third are bad, but are possible after a chord on an accented beat.

(*d*) Roots falling a third are good.

(*e*) Roots rising a second are good after IV and V, and possible in the major mode after I and III.

(*f*) Roots falling a second are generally bad, except VI to V.

The immediate repetition of a chord, though not actually a progression, is good at the commencement of a passage, and after a chord on an accented beat.

---

* Sometimes termed the dominant progression.

The term 'bad' when used in reference to harmonic progressions signifies a somewhat weak succession of chords; it does not necessarily imply an incorrect progression. All diatonic progressions are possible, and even those termed 'bad' may be employed with good effect in certain cas s.

The following example illustrates the harmonic progressions in relation to the chord of C; roots falling a second, however, are omitted, as Lo will for the present be avoided.

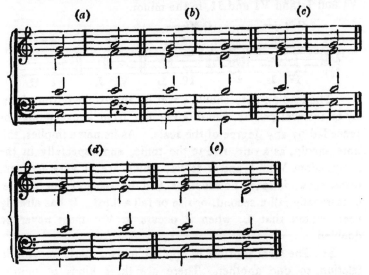

40. The term movement is applied to the interval between the two notes of a melodic progression. The movement is said to be conjunct (or, by 'step') when the interval is a second, as in a *scale* passage; and it is said to be disjunct (or, by 'skip') when the interval is greater than a second, as in an *arpeggio* passage.

The melodic movement of the upper parts should, as a rule, be as smooth as possible; and when a note is common to both chords of a progression t is generally best to retain it in the same part for both chords. The melodic interval of a third and that of a fourth may often be employed, and occasionally even that of a fifth, but the skip of a sixth is rarely advisable, while that of a seventh is forbidden altogether. The skip of an octave is allowed, at the same time this interval does not often occur in connection with the common chord in root position.

The *augmented* intervals, being somewhat difficult to sing should be avoided. Augmented intervals naturally occur between IV and L in the major mode, and between IV and L, VI and L., and VI and II, in the minor.

The leading-note should never be approached from *below* by an interval *greater than a third*; but from above it may be preceded by any degree of the scale. As its name implies, this note should, as a rule, rise to the tonic, and especially in the progressions V to I and V to VI, which are of very frequent occurrence; it may, however, as will be seen in due course, occasionally fall a second, or rise or fall a third. It has already been stated that L, when it occurs in V+ must never be doubled.

41. The term **motion** is applied to two parts moving in relation to one another. There are three kinds of motion possible between any two parts, viz., **similar,** when they move in the same direction; **contrary,** when they move in opposite directions; and **oblique,** when one part remains stationary, the other part moving.

No two parts at the interval of a perfect fifth or octave (or unison) in one chord are allowed to proceed to the same interval in the succeeding chord. Such progressions are commonly called **consecutive fifths and octaves ;*** they are *absolutely prohibited*, and must be *avoided at all costs*. The following progressions are, therefore, all incorrect; at *a*, there are consecutive fifths between the bass and tenor; at *b*, between the bass and treble; in this case the consecutives are compound fifths, but they are just as objectionable as the simple intervals; at *c*, there are consecutive octaves between the bass and tenor; and at *d*, there are consecutive fifths between the alto and treble, with consecutive octaves between the bass and alto, and consequently consecutive compound fifths between the bass and treble.

The chords in the above progressions, as individual chords, are all *correctly written*; the bass is doubled in every case, and each chord is in either close or open position. The effect of a progression, therefore, does not depend upon the effect of the constituent chords, it depends, in the first place, upon the *movement* of each individual part, and, in the second place, upon the *motion* between any two parts in relation to one another.

In the following progression, at *e*, there is a perfect fifth between the tenor and alto in the first chord, and between the bass and tenor in the second; there is also an octave between the bass and tenor of the first chord, and an octave between

---

* Sometimes termed Parallel fifths and octaves.

the bass and treble of the second; no bad effect, however,
arises in this case, as the fifths and the octaves do not occur
between the *same* parts.

Neither is there any bad effect from the consecutive fifths
and octaves which arise when a chord is *repeated*, as at *f*.

Consecutives, when introduced by contrary motion, as
exemplified by the octaves between the bass and treble at *g*,
are not as objectionable as direct consecutives, but they should
only be employed in order to produce some particular effect, a
consideration which need not enter into the early academic
work of the student of harmony.

(g)

Consecutive octaves are permitted in compositions when their purpose is *to strengthen a melody*; and both consecutive fitfhs and octaves *may* be employed by contrary motion, when the roots of the two chords move a perfect fourth or fifth. Consecutive thirds and sixths may be freely employed; consecutive fourths between the upper parts, but not between the bass and an upper part, may also be freely employed. Consecutive seconds and sevenths are forbidden, but these evidently cannot occur in connection with common chords.

Although consecutive fifths are occasionally to be found in the works of the great composers, yet they occur, it may be said, more frequently in instrumental than in vocal compositions, and while their presence indicates that under certain conditions they are not objectionable, it by no means justifies their use by students.

42. The motion between *the extreme parts* requires special consideration, for not only are direct consecutive fifths and octaves forbidden, but even similar motion to a perfect fifth or octave (between the treble and bass), except in the case of certain progressions shortly to be explained, is also disallowed Motion of this character gives rise to what is termed **hidden consecutives.***

The following progressions are all bad; at *a* and *b* there are hidden fifths, and àt *c* and *d* hidden octaves, between the extreme parts. It should be noticed that the treble moves *disjunctly* in each case.

The *hidden* consecutives may be discovered by inserting the intervening diatonic notes.

When the roots move a perfect fourth or fifth, except alone in the progression II to V, provided the treble moves one degree only, hidden consecutives rarely produce a bad effect

---

* Sometimes called concealed or covered consecutives.

and especially is this the case when both chords are *primary triads* (§ 34). The following progressions, therefore, are all good; at *e* and *f* there are hidden fifths, and at *g* and *h* hidden octaves, between the extreme parts. It will be noticed that the treble here moves *conjunctly* in each case.

In the progression II to V, it is generally best to let the upper parts *fall*, especially when the *third* of II is in the treble. The hidden octaves at *i*, even though the treble moves conjunctly, are *not good*; while the hidden fifths at *j*, notwithstanding that the treble moves disjunctly, are *not bad*. It must be remembered that this is the only case in which similar motion between the extreme parts to a perfect fifth, *with a skip in the treble*, is allowed. When the *fifth* of II is in the treble, it often rises, as shown at *k*. In the rarely employed progression V to II, it is generally best to let the treble take contrary motion with the bass, as shown at *l*.

43. If the following suggestions are complied with, consecutive fifths and octaves are *impracticable*. The chords in every case should be complete, the bass being doubled; the

second chord should be in the same position, close or open, as the first; and the movement should invariably be to the nearest possible note.

1. When the roots move a second, let the upper parts take contrary motion with the bass; an important exception, however, to this rule will be found in § 45.

2. When the roots move a third, let two of the upper parts take oblique motion, and let the other part take contrary motion.

3. When the roots move a fourth, let the note common to the two chords be retained in the same part, and let the other notes move in similar motion (one degree only).

4. When the roots move a fifth, let the note common to the two chords be retained in the same part, and let the other parts move in contrary motion (one degree only).

5. When the roots move a sixth—a rare progression—let the treble and one of the other parts take oblique motion, and let the other part move in similar motion (one degree only).

When the roots move an octave, the upper parts may remain stationary, or may move in either similar or contrary motion; the position also may be changed from close to open, or vice versa; while hidden consecutive fifths and octaves do not produce a bad effect.

The above suggestions are not to be regarded absolutely as rules, at the same time the student will do well to follow them in writing his early exercises. Each progression may, as a matter of fact, be harmonized in a variety of ways, but the student, at first, will do well to work upon some definite principles, such as the above, and when he has acquired the ability to harmonize progressions correctly in one way, and not till then, he should practise harmonizing them in other ways.

It has already been stated (§ 36) that the parts should not *cross* one another; it may now be added, that except under certain conditions they also should not **overlap** one another. Overlapping is the crossing of parts in the course of a progression; it occurs when one part proceeds to a higher or lower note in the second chord than that which an approximate part took in the first chord. Thus, at *a*, the bass in the second chord takes F, a higher note than the E which the tenor took in the first chord;

again, at *b*, the treble in the second chord takes G, a lower note than the A which the alto took in the first chord; the alto at the same time taking a lower note in the second chord than that which the tenor took in the first. Overlapping, however, is not objectionable between the tenor and bass, when, as at *c*, the tenor, taking L, rises a semitone while the bass rises a perfect fourth, V to I.

Although the overlapping of parts is forbidden, as a general rule, yet it may be freely employed, especially between the inner parts, should the purpose be to avoid the infringement of a more important rule.

44. In the following examples, the progressions from the chord of C to each of the other chords in the key of C are illustrated, each progression being harmonized in various ways. Roots *rising* are alone exemplified, but the progressions in each case may be reversed, when the harmonization of roots *falling* to the tonic will be obtained. The progressions at *a* (in close position) and at *b* (in open position) are written in accordance with the suggestions in § 43; at *c*, the third of the first chord moves in similar motion with the bass to the third of the second, the other parts taking contrary motion in order to avoid consecutives; at *d*, the first chord is incomplete, for, with G in the tenor there would be consecutive fifths with the bass; at *e*, the first chord is in open position and the second in close [1]; at *f*, the first chord is incomplete, G being omitted in the tenor, in order that all the parts should not proceed simultaneously by similar motion [2]; at *g*, the first chord is incomplete for two reasons, viz., G is

omitted in the tenor in order to avoid overlapping with the bass, and it is omitted in the alto in order to avoid consecutive fifths by contrary motion with the bass.

(1) The student must exercise great care in changing from open to close position; in so doing consecutives are very liable to occur.

(2) It is rarely productive of a good effect when chords are in root position, except perhaps in the case of harmonic repetition, for all parts to proceed by similar motion.

1. Roots moving a second.

2. Roots moving a third.

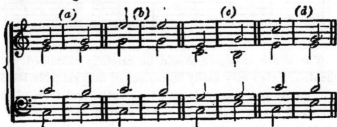

3. Roots moving a fourth.

4. Roots moving a fifth.

5. Roots moving a sixth.

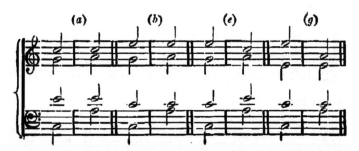

The above examples should be carefully examined by the student, and they may easily be converted into valuable lessons; thus, 1, write out the treble and bass parts, and then, (without referring to the example) add alto and tenor parts; 2, write the bass only; 3, the treble only; 4, the alto; 5, the tenor; and then add the three other parts. The examples may also be transposed up or down a major or a minor second.

Of the three kinds of motion, it may be said that contrary (rather than similar or oblique) is the best, as a rule, between the extreme parts; it not only produces the boldest effects, but, speaking generally, it is also the safest in the matter of avoiding consecutives. There are, however, two cases when it should not be employed.

(*a*) When the roots fall a third, contrary motion in the treble to the fifth of the second chord is undesirable.

(*b*) In the somewhat rare progression V to IV, it is objectionable to place L rising to I in the treble.

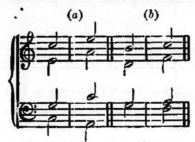

45. It has already been stated (§ 38) that **the leading note** (L) *must not be doubled.* This rule is absolute when L occurs in V ; when L occurs in another chord, such as III, the rule is not so stringent. The most frequently employed and, therefore, the most important progressions from V are to I and to VI ; in each of these progressions the part which takes L should, as a rule, rise to I, and especially is this the case when L occurs in the treble. This treatment of L in the progression V to I, is shown at *a* ; when as at *b*, L occurs in the tenor, with II falling to I in the treble, it is customary to omit the fifth in I ; it is not incorrect, however, for L to descend, as at *c*, when it is in an inner part, provided that it moves in contrary motion with the bass ; in order to employ I in its complete form, the fifth may be omitted in V, as shown at *d*.

The following example is a transcription of the above progressions into the key of C minor.

In the progression V to VI, L rising to I, in similar motion
with the bass moving a second, necessitates the doubling of the
third in VI, as shown at *e* and *i*; for the other parts must take
contrary motion with the bass in order to avoid consecutive fifths
and octaves. When L is in an inner part in the major mode
it sometimes falls as at *f*, but in the minor mode, L must rise to
I in order to avoid the movement by an augmented second (§ 40),
as shown in the alto at *j* The progression VI to V, in the
major mode may be written as at *g*, but in the minor mode the
augmented second would again appear, this time in the treble, as
at *k*; to avoid this interval, it is necessary to double the third in
VI, as at *l*; and, indeed, the third is frequently doubled in VI,
when this progression occurs in the major mode, as shown at *h*.

46. **To harmonize a given melodic progression** occurring in the treble, alto or tenor, it is necessary in the first place to determine the chords to which each note, taken separately, belongs (see § 38), and in the second place to choose those roots which will give the best harmonic progressions (see § 39) ; after which the other parts may be added in accordance with the laws for part-writing given above.

In the following melodic progression

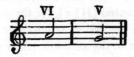

VI occurs in the triads VI –, IV + and II – ; and V in the triads V +, III – and I + ; there are, therefore, nine possible progressions in all, and these are illustrated in the following example.

The progression at *a* is impracticable on account of the consecutive octaves, and likewise that at *i* on account of the consecutive fifths; the progressions at *b*, *f* and *g*, (roots moving a
perfect fourth or fifth) are all good; the progression at *d* is also
good; that at *c* is possible; while those at *e* and *h* are bad.

In reference to the progressions at *e* and *h*, it may here be
said that there is a peculiar harshness attached to the triad on
the mediant, and it can rarely be employed with good effect
except after V or VI. In the minor mode the triad on the
mediant being augmented (III×), for the present will not be employed at all. Since the two most important chords in a key are
the tonic and dominant, the aesthetic effect of these chords being
respectively *rest* and *motion*; and since the characteristic note of
a chord is its third (hence the rule against omitting the third of a
chord), so the reason for the unpleasant effect in connection with
the mediant chord is probably due to the fact that this chord
contains the characteristic notes of the tonic and dominant
chords, the clashing relationship of which is especially noticeable
in the augmented triad of the minor mode.

As the special purpose of the above example is to illustrate
the possible harmonies for the given melodic progressions, the
chords are not completed; the other parts may be added in two
ways, either by regarding the upper notes of each progression as
the treble, and then adding an alto and tenor, employing close
position; or by regarding the upper notes as the alto, and then
adding a treble and tenor, employing open position.

In working exercises on harmonic progressions, the student
must not rest satisfied with having written the individual chords
correctly, but he must, furthermore, examine the movement of
the various parts both separately and in relation to one another,
always avoiding consecutive fifths and octaves, objectionable
hidden consecutives, augmented intervals and unnecessarily
large skips, crossing and overlapping the parts, doubling or
omitting notes unadvisably, and incorrect treatment of the leading-note. These are the principal mistakes which the beginner

in harmony is apt to make, and they should be scrupulously
guarded against from the very first; the student should feel satisfied that his progressions are correct before submitting them to
the scrutiny of the teacher; by so doing, a certain sense of confidence in his own powers will quickly be established, which, in
due course, will not only enable him to acquire with ease the art
of part writing, but will also kindle a love for the subject, and in
all probability lead him ultimately into the realm of musical
composition.

SUMMARY.

§ 39. The harmonic progressions.

Roots rising a third and falling a second, except VI to V,
generally bad.

§ 40. Movement, conjunct and disjunct.

Augmented intervals to be avoided; movement to and
from L.

§ 41. Motion, similar, contrary and oblique.

Consecutive fifths and octaves (unisons) to be avoided.

§ 42. Motion between the extreme parts.

Hidden consecutive fifths and octaves, except under
certain conditions, are objectionable.

§ 43. Suggestions for the avoidance of consecutives.

Crossing and overlapping of the parts forbidden.

§ 44. Progressions from the chord of C.

If carefully studied these should be valuable lessons.

§ 45. The treatment of L in the progressions V to I and
V to VI.

Generally best for L to rise to I, especially when in the
treble.

§ 46. The harmonization of a melodic progression in the
treble.

The peculiar character of the mediant chord. Summary of
faults to be avoided; the importance of correct work
in early exercises.

EXERCISES.

I

Add alto and tenor parts to the following progressions ; employ close position in No. 1, and open position in No. 2.*

*The student must be careful in writing the notes which have stems. In close score (also called piano score) the treble and tenor stems are turned *up*, the alto and bass turned *down*. In open (or vocal) score the stems are turned according to the position of the notes on the stave, those above the middle line being turned down, and vice versa.

3. Distinguish between 'movement' and 'motion,' and give examples of each in the key of A.

4. Name the *movement* in the treble, and the *motion* between the extreme parts, in each of the following progressions; also state the *position* of each chord.

5. Explain the meaning of *hidden* consecutive fifths and octaves; and state when their effect is good and when bad. Criticize the motion between the extreme parts in the following progressions.

6. Explain the difference between *crossing* and *overlapping* of parts. Under what conditions is the latter allowed?

7. Discover the mistakes in the following progressions.

Add treble, alto and tenor parts to the following progressions, working each in both close and open position.

10. Add alto and tenor parts to the following progressions.

In the above exercise special care must be taken to avoid consecutives, awkward skips in the middle parts, etc. ; it is often more troublesome to harmonize a progression in which the treble is given than one in which it is not given.

11. State the rules regarding the Leading-note ; explain the treatment of this note in progressions which contain the chord of the dominant, and give examples in the key of A minor.

12. Add treble, alto and tenor parts to the following progressions ; each progression should be worked twice in close and twice in open position.

For the purpose of practice, many of the above exercises may be worked in other ways ; thus, in No. 1, the treble may be changed and the chords harmonized in open position ; similarly No. 2 may be worked in close position ; or both exercises may be transposed up or down a second or third ; while each progression may be harmonized in six or eight different ways, as shown in No. 4.

II.

13. Write, in the key of E flat, the progressions:
(a) I+ to V+, (b) IV+ to II−, (c) V+ to VI−, (d) IV+ to I+.

14. Write, in the key of F sharp minor, the progressions:
(a) I− to IV−, (b) VI+ to IV−, (c) IV− to V+, (d) V+ to I−.

Complete the following progressions by adding in Nos. 15 and 16, a *succeeding* chord, and in Nos. 17 and 18, a *preceding* chord; the same root movement not to be employed twice in any one exercise.

15. *E Major.*

16. *C sharp minor.*

17. *A flat major.*

18. *F minor.*

Add alto, tenor and bass parts to the following melodic progressions, working each in two or three different ways.

19.

20.

Harmonize the following melodic progressions; in No. 21 add treble, tenor and bass parts; in No. 22 add treble, alto and bass parts. Write in open score.

21.

22.

23. Write three good progressions in the bass in the keys of E major and F minor, and then add the upper parts.

24. Write, commencing with the tonic, three simple progressions in the treble in the keys of D major and B minor, and then add the lower parts.

CHAPTER VI.

CADENCES, SEQUENCES, ETC.

47. Musical compositions consist of *continuous* harmonic progressions, each chord (except, of course, the first and the last) being in definite relationship with the chords which immediately *precede* and *follow* it.

The simplest form of composition, such as the hymn tune, the ballad melody, etc., is called a **musical sentence.** The *normal* sentence, also called a *period*, is eight measures in length, and is divisible into two equal portions, called *phrases*. The concluding harmonic progression of each phrase is called a *cadence* (Lat. *Cado*, I fall).

Cadences are divided into two classes, the Regular and the Irregular.

Regular cadences are also divided into two classes, the *Perfect* and the *Imperfect*. Perfect cadences conclude with the *tonic* chord, imperfect with the *dominant* chord. Irregular cadences are those which conclude with other chords.

The perfect cadence is of two kinds, viz., the *Authentic*, in which I is preceded by V, as at *a* and *b*, and the *Plagal*, in which I is preceded by IV, as at *c* and *d.*

In the imperfect cadence V is usually preceded by I, as at *e* and *f*, but it may be preceded by any chord which does not contain L, as at *g* and *h*.

Of the irregular cadences the most important is that at *i*, V to VI, known as the *Deceptive* cadence*; another irregular

---

* The terms Interrupted, False and Broken are also applied to this cadence; the term Deceptive, however, seems the most suitable, for V naturally proceeds to I, and when in place of this it proceeds to VI, the listener who expects the natural progression is certainly deceived. The term Interrupted, in the present work, will be employed to indicate an incomplete cadence, one in which the second chord is omitted altogether, its place being taken by a rest.

cadence is that at *j*, I to IV, sometimes called the subdominant cadence. Roots falling a third, as at *k* and *l*, do not constitute very satisfactory cadences; they are, however, sometimes employed. Other irregular cadences will be considered in due course.

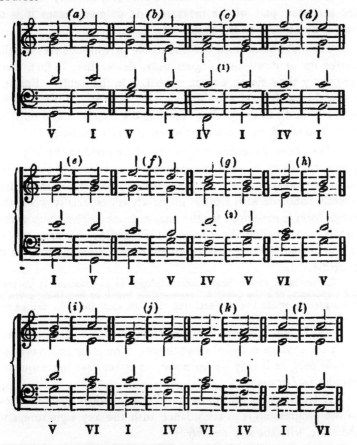

1. Sometimes called the Church cadence, as it is more frequently employed in sacred than in secular music.

2. Sometimes called the Mixed cadence, on the ground that it is a mixture of the plagal and imperfect cadences.

The authentic form of the perfect cadence is employed at the *close* of almost every composition; it is indeed, commonly called the perfect cadence; it is also called by some authorities a full close, the imperfect being called a half close.

The second chord of a cadence almost invariably falls upon the accented part of the measure, and in many cases it is of longer duration than the first.

It should be noticed that the treble part in cadences usually moves up or down one degree only, descending, in fact, more frequently than rising, except when L is in the treble. Furthermore, the treble part should invariably end on I (preceded by either II or L) in the perfect cadence, if a complete and finished effect is desired, as at the conclusion of a composition.

The above cadences may all be transcribed to the key of C minor, the effect of each cadence being the same in the minor as in the major mode. Compositions in the minor mode frequently conclude with a tonic major chord, especially when the plagal form is employed for the final cadence. The tonic chord in this case is called the **Tierce de Picardie;** the progression, it is presumed, having had its origin in the French province of Picardie.

Cadences in music bear some analogy to punctuation in poetry ; the imperfect, like the comma, represents a break or breathing point in the sentence, while the perfect, like the full stop (period), brings the sentence to a conclusion.

48. When a given progression is repeated at a different pitch the passage is called a **sequence.** The progression may be *melodic* only, or it may be *harmonic*; in either case the sequence may be *real* or *tonal.*

A sequence is said to be **tonal** (see *a*) when the repetition of the progression is in accordance with the key signature, and therefore, with the key *tonality.*

A sequence is said to be **real** (see *b*) when the repetition of the progression, in the matter of both its melodic and harmonic intervals, is *exact*; and this necessitates a change of key at each recurrence of the progression.

The first progression in the above sequences is called the **model.** A model may consist of two, three, or, at the most, four chords, the sequence being termed duple, triple, or quadruple accordingly. In each of the above examples the model is repeated at the second above. The sequence itself is said to be formed by roots rising a fourth and falling a third.

The most important sequence of common chords occurs when the roots alternately rise a fourth, and fall a fifth; this will be known as **the dominant sequence;** it is open to much variety in treatment, as will be seen later, in conjunction with chords of the seventh.

49. In order to preserve a sequence it is often necessary to employ the diminished triad, and sometimes, even the augmented triad, IIIx of the minor mode; the melodic use of augmented intervals is not altogether objectionable, though they should be avoided as far as possible in the treble.   The fifth in the diminished and augmented triads being dissonant, requires special treatment, technically termed *resolution*; in the diminished triad the fifth resolves by *descending* one degree (in the same part) in the next chord (see *a*), or possibly in the next but one (see *b*); while the fifth in the augmented triad resolves by *ascending* one degree (see *c*).

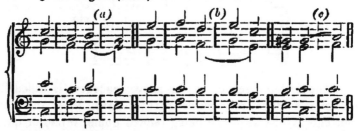

In an ascending sequence, the fifth of the diminished triad is allowed to *ascend*.   In a descending sequence, in the minor mode, a minor chord on the dominant (V − instead of V +) is often employed in order to avoid the augmented second.

50. In addition to the rules for writing melodic progressions which have already been given (§ 40), the following injunctions and exceptions refer to *continuous* progressions.

(1) After the skip of a diminished interval the melody should return at once to a note within that interval, as at *a* and *c*, and not as at *b* and *d*.

(2) Two skips in the same direction forming the interval of a seventh, as at *e* and *f*, should be avoided; these skips, however, are tolerable in rising to and from the tonic, as at *g*.

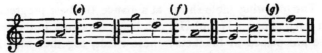

(3) Two skips forming an octave are good if one is a perfect fourth and the other a perfect fifth, as at *h* and *i*, but they are objectionable if one is a third and the other a sixth, as at *j* and *k*. Two skips forming an interval greater than an octave are forbidden,

(4) The skip of a sixth, though it should generally be avoided, is good when introduced as at *l*, and possible as at *m*; in each case it should be noticed that the skip is upwards. This skip is good only after I and V.

(5) The skip of an augmented second is least objectionable when it occurs in a short scale passage, and in an inner part, as at *n* and *o*.

(6) The skip of an augmented fourth, as has already been seen, is permissible in sequences only.

51. Continuous harmonic progressions are written in accordance with the root progressions as given in § 39; it is, however, necessary to arrange the chords so that they form a correct musical sentence.

The following table shows at a glance the best progressions
from each chord; II and III, not being concords in the minor
mode are placed in brackets; these triads, together with L in
both modes, should be employed only when they can be correctly
resolved (§ 49); in the early exercises it would be well to avoid
their use altogether.   This table should be read upwards.

L	may proceed to	I	(III)			
VI	"	"	(II)	(III)	IV	V
V	"	"	I	(II)	(III)	VI
IV	"	"	I	(II)	V	L
(III)	"	"	I	IV	VI	L
(II)	"	"	V	VI	L	
I	"	"	(II)	IV	V	VI

Roots rising a third, through rarely good in effect, may be
employed occasionally; they are generally most effective after a
chord on an accented beat.   The progression V to IV is also
possible, provided L is not placed in the treble.   The progression
V to II, although it is given in the above table, seldom has a good
effect.   The repetition of a chord is good if the chord is first
heard on a strong beat, and possible, though rarely effective, after
a chord on a weak beat.

52. The normal form of the musical sentence may be represented thus:—

The above is called a *blank rhythm*.   The notes bracketed
indicate the position of the cadences; the first is usually an imperfect cadence, the second is necessarily a perfect cadence.
The above blank rhythm may be clothed with harmony by writing, in the first place, a bass (*a*) in accordance with the above
table, and in the second place, by adding (to this bass) the upper
parts (*b*) in accordance with the rules given in the preceding
chapter.

(a)

The first cadence in the above passage, which may be termed a melodic sentence, has been purposely chosen because it is frequently employed in the major mode ; in the minor mode, II is a diminished triad, for which reason this cadence was not included in the examples given in § 47. In the following example the passage is converted into a complete musical sentence.

(b)

53. The *simplest* form of the musical sentence in actual use is the short, but at the same time, complete composition known as the **Anglican chant.** The construction of this chant is shown in the following blank rhythm.

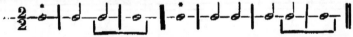

The notes in the above rhythm which are marked with an asterisk indicate what are called the notes or chords of *recitation*; in chanting, these chords have no definite time value, but they are always represented by whole notes. The second chord of recitation, it may be said, should in no case be a repetition of the first.

The first cadence in an Anglican chant is left entirely to the taste of the composer, but the second cadence must be perfect, either authentic or plagal.

The following are illustrative examples of this form of composition, No. 1 in C major, No. 2 in C minor. At *a*, roots
rising a third after a chord upon an accented beat are employed;
the cadence at *b*, is a form of the imperfect cadence (see *h*, § 47);
for the second chord of recitation, *c*, the somewhat rarely
employed III - is introduced;. at *d*, the subdominant cadence is
employed (see *j*, § 47); roots rising a sixth are exemplified at *e*;
the disjunct movement in the treble in similar motion with the
bass at this point, is good, since the upper part moves to the
third of the root.

The Anglican chant is an example of an *irregular* musical
sentence, the first section being a contracted phrase. The
double bar in the middle of the chant in no way affects the
harmonic progression at this point; it simply divides the chant
into two parts, just as the verses of a Psalm are divided into two
parts by a colon, the double bar corresponding with the colon.
The brevity of this little composition led to the invention of the
double chant, which is exactly twice the length of the single
chant, and contains, therefore, four cadences.

54. Since there are but six common chords in the major key, and only four in the minor (see § 33), in order to obtain variety of effects in the matter of harmonic progressions, and to avoid the fault known as *monotonous tonality*, it is necessary to *modulate*, that is to say, to pass into a new key.

Every key is closely related to certain other keys, called *attendant* keys; these are, the relative of the given key, the dominant and its relative, and the subdominant and its relative.

The **attendant keys** of C major and A minor will be seen from the following table:—

Subdominant.	Tonic.	Dominant.
F major.	C major. —or—	G major.
D minor.	A minor.	E minor.

It may also be said that the signature of an attendant key never contains more than one sharp or flat, more or less, than the given key.

The attendant keys may easily be remembered from the following passages, in which the half-notes represent the tonics of the given keys, while the quarter-notes represent the tonics of the attendant keys.

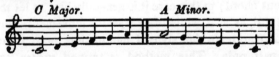

55. A modulation to an *attendant* key may be effected by employing a chord that is common to the two keys; this chord, called the *ambiguous* chord, being *introduced* as belonging to the first key, and *quitted* as belonging to the second; after which a perfect cadence is necessary to establish definitely the new key. This method of proceeding to a new key is termed *gradual* modulation. In the following example, modulations are made to all the attendant keys of C major:—

* Ambiguous chords.

In major keys the first modulation is generally to the *dominant*, and in minor keys to the *relative major*. The new tonic chord almost invariably appears upon an accented beat.

56. A modulation may be effected *unexpectedly*, the dominant chord of the new key being introduced without any ambiguous chord; in this case it is generally best to let the roots move a third, as at *a*, while the *chromatic* movement, which is an important feature in this style of modulation, must be confined to one part only. This method is termed *sudden* or *abrupt* modulation.

The chromatic movement in the above example, it will be seen, is in the alto. When this movement is not confined to one part, as in the following example at *b*, the fault known as **False relation** arises, the E flat in the treble of the second chord being in false relation with the E natural in the alto of the first chord. To avoid the false relation this progression should be written as at *c* or *d*.

Furthermore, the bad effect of the false relation is often present even though an intervening chord, as at *e*, is introduced. When, however, a composition in the minor mode concludes with the Tierce de Picardie (§ 47), no bad effect arises from the false relation, whether the cadence is perfect, as at *f*, or plagal, as at *g*.

In the first of the above examples, at *a*, there is no bad effect from the false relation between the F in the bass of the second chord and the F sharp in the alto of the third ; the chromatic movement could not occur in two parts simultaneously, as it would give rise to consecutive octaves.

False relation, it may here be said, does not invariably produce a bad effect ; it is occasionally to be found in the works of the older masters, and is of common occurrence in modern compositions ; at the same time the student, especially in his early exercises, should avoid it altogether.

57. Compositions in the minor mode, even those of the simplest character (except perhaps the Anglican chant), almost invariably contain a modulation, usually to the key of the relative major. The reason for the frequent change of tonality in this case is due to the paucity of the harmonic progressions in the minor mode, it being impossible to obtain much variety in effect from the use of only four common chords.

Furthermore, and chiefly in order to avoid the melodic movement of an augmented second, certain **additional** chords are occasionally employed in the minor mode; these chords are formed by the use of +VI (the major submediant) and VII (the subtonic) instead of −VI and L.; and since one of these notes is found in every triad in the key except that on the tonic, there are consequently six of these additional triads. At *A* the triads derived from the *harmonic* form of the minor scale are shown (see also § 33); at *B* the triads derived from the *melodic* form of the minor scale are shown.

A.

I−   IIo   III×   IV−   V+   VI+   Lo

B.

(a)   (b)   (c)   (d)   (e)   (f)   (g)

I−   II−   III+   IV+   V−   +VIo   VII+

The tonic triad, *a*, is always employed in the minor form, except alone when it occurs at the close of a composition as the Tierce de Picardie. The additional triads are regarded as '*borrowed*' chords; the triads at *b* and *d* being borrowed from the tonic major key; those at *c*, *e* and *g*, from the relative major; the rarely employed diminished triad at *f*, from the dominant of the relative major. The triads, III+, V− and VII+ are more frequently employed than the others; they usually occur in descending passages, and especially in falling sequences, as exemplified at *h* and *i*.

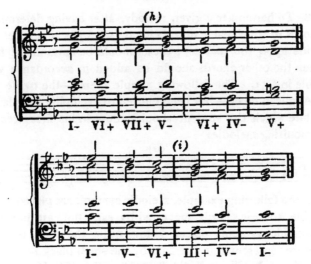

I- VI+ VII+ V-   VI+ IV-   V+

I-   V- VI+ III+ IV-   I-

IV+ and +VIo are rarely employed in their root position, the latter being a diminished triad and the former almost invariably giving rise to a feeling of dubious tonality. II - is a valuable chord when the leading-note is approached from the major submediant, as in the treble at *i*, and in the tenor at *k*.

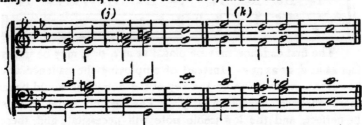

The best progressions both to and from the additional triads may be gathered from the table in § 51, each triad being considered as temporarily belonging to the key from which it is regarded as being borrowed.

The student is strongly advised to exercise the greatest care in the employment of these triads; he should thoroughly master the progressions to and from the principal triads of the (harmonic) minor mode, and should employ the add'tional triads only when their presence can unquestionably be justified.

58. To harmonize a given melody, after having determined
the chords to which each note belongs (see § 38), it is necessary
to decide upon the *cadences*; these should be harmonized first,
and then the other chords should be added in accordance with
the table in § 51.   The following simple theme—the treble part
of an Anglican chant—has been chosen to exemplify the plan of
procedure which the student should adopt in his first attempts
at harmonizing melodies.

In the following example, melodic symbols are placed above
the treble, and the chords suggested by each note are indicated
by harmonic symbols placed below, while the roots of these
chords are represented in the bass by the small black notes.

The first cadence may be plagal as at *c*, or it may be imperfect as at *d*, or as at *e*.   Instead of employing the cadence at *e*,
however, a modulation to the key of the dominant would be far
more effective, as shown at *f*.   The second cadence must
be perfect, and the low treble note will necessitate and, therefore, justify a correspondingly low tenor note.

The following examples are varied harmonizations of this chant.

The harmonic progressions in the above chants should be carefully examined; but the only chord to which particular attention must be directed, is the mediant, as employed in the fore phrase in both the chants *A* and *B*. This chord as here introduced is effective, notwithstanding that it occurs upon an accented beat; this is due to the conjunct movement in the treble, together with the contrary motion between the extreme parts.

When the student has worked the exercises at the end of the present chapter, he should compose several Anglican chants in various major and minor keys, making them as melodious and as interesting as possible. A little practice will enable him to master this simple form of composition, and at the same time he will become perfectly familiar with the best harmonic progressions ; he will also learn how few good progressions there really are in connection with the common chord ; while in due course he will naturally crave for other chords, for, music consisting of the common chord constantly employed in root position only, possesses a character of what may be termed 'stilted severity.'

SUMMARY.

§ 47. Cadences.

Regular { Perfect, ending on I, Authentic and Plagal.
{ Imperfect, ending on V.

Irregular, all others, the most important being the Deceptive.

§ 48. Sequences.

Melodic and harmonic ; real and tonal. The dominant sequence.

§ 49. The dissonant triads.

5 × resolves by ascending, 5 o by descending.

§ 50. Melodic progressions (continuous).

Various injunctions and exceptions.

§ 51. Harmonic progressions (continuous).

The table should be committed to memory.

§ 52. The Normal sentence.

Eight measures in length, divided into two phrases, each of which concludes with a cadence.

§ 53. The Anglican chant.

An irregular sentence ; the simplest form of composition.

§ 54. The Attendant keys.

IV and V, and the relatives of I, IV and V.

§ 55. Modulation—gradual.

The ambiguous chord.

§ 56. Modulation—sudden.

The chromatic change. False relation to be avoided.

§ 57. The additional triads of the minor mode.

Their special purpose being to avoid the augmented second.

§ 58. The harmonization of a melody.

First determine the cadences, then choose the best harmonic progressions.

EXERCISES.

I.

Add alto and tenor parts to the following :—

1.

2.

In working these and all future exercises, the student should invariably place the correct symbol under each bass-note ; by so doing he will not only the more readily recognise the various chords as they occur in the different keys, but he will insensibly also memorize the progressions, and this will be invaluable to him both in harmonizing melodies and in composing simple musical sentences.

Add treble, alto and tenor parts to the following basses:—

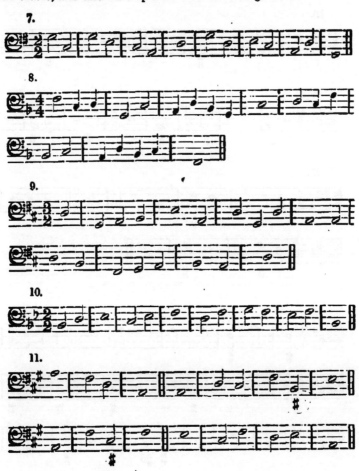

12.

13.

14.

15.

16.

17. Name the following cadences :—

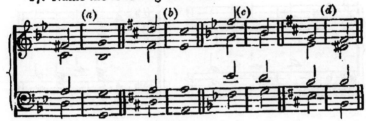

18. Write the following cadences :—

(a) Perfect (Authentic) in C sharp minor.

(b) Imperfect in A flat.

(c) Imperfect (Mixed) in E.

(d) Plagal, with Tierce de Picardie, in F minor.

(e) Deceptive in E flat major and in F sharp minor.

19. Write short tonal sequences, each three measures in length, on the following models.

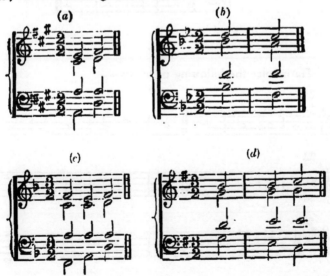

In no case should the model be repeated at an interval greater than a third.

20. Continue the following real (dominant) sequence, passing through all the major keys, and concluding with a chord of C.

II.

Harmonize the following melodies :—

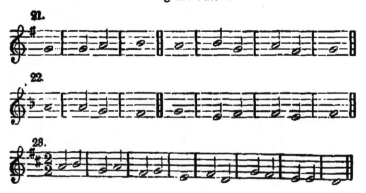

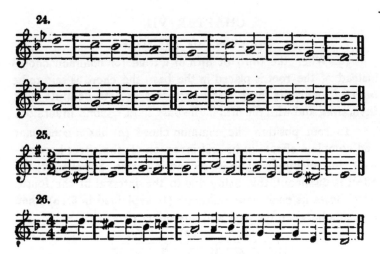

Clothe the following blank rhythms with harmony, introducing cadences at the bracketed notes.

29. Compose a musical sentence in the key of G. Write the bass first.

30. Write a short passage in the key of D minor.

When, as above, the exercises are divided into two groups, those in Group II may, if preferred, be omitted when the chapter is first studied, and may be worked later on when the chapter is being reviewed.

CHAPTER VII.

THE CHORD OF THE SIXTH.

59. When the third or fifth of a triad (or common chord) instead of the root is placed in the bass, the chord is said to be *inverted*; with the third in the bass, it is said to be in its **first inversion**, and with the fifth in the bass, in its **second inversion.**

In root position the common chord (*a*) has a consonant and complete effect; in its first inversion (*b*) the effect is consonant, but incomplete; in its second inversion, however, (*c*) the effect is dissonant, this being due to the interval of the fourth which loses its consonant character (as explained in § 19) when it occurs between the bass and any upper part.

In order to distinguish between the root position and the inversions of the chord, **figures** representing the *intervals* between the bass and the upper notes are placed immediately below (or sometimes above) the bass part; hence the expression **Figured-bass,** from which arose the term Thorough-bass, the name by which harmony was formerly known.

The **first inversion** is figured $\frac{6}{3}$, which, however, is usually contracted to 6, the 3 being understood; the second inversion is figured $\frac{6}{4}$. The *root* of **a chord of the sixth,** as the first inversion is generally called, is a third below the bass-note; the *root* of a six-four chord is a fifth below the bass.

Inverted chords may be named either from the bass-note or from the root; for example the chord at *b* may be regarded as a sixth on the mediant, or as the first inversion of the tonic chord; likewise the chord at *c* may be regarded as a six-four on the dominant, or as the second inversion of the tonic chord.

The **symbols** for inverted chords are formed by placing a
mall Arabic figure, indicating the inversions, immediately after
the Roman numeral employed for the root. Thus, the symbol
for the chord at *b*, above, is I[1], and for that at *c*, I[2]; or, if it is
desirable to represent the (major) character of these chords, the
symbols would be I + [1] and I + [2] respectively. I – [1] and I – [2] are
the symbols for the inversions of a tonic minor chord. The
symbol for the first inversion of the diminished triad on the leading-note is Lo[1], but this may be contracted to L.[1], as the triad on
L is *always* diminished. The o, however, must not be omitted
from the symbol IIo[1], employed for the first inversion of the
diminished triad on the supertonic of the minor mode.

60. In the first inversion of the common chord the bass-
note, as a rule, should *not be doubled*, especially if the root is
either I, IV or V. It is generally best to *double the note employed
for the treble.*

I[1] may be harmonized in any of the following ways :—

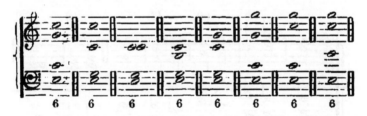

Of the above chords, though the position is good in each,
yet the positions at *a* and *e* are to be preferred; the position of a
chord of the sixth, however, depends entirely upon the context,
that is to say, the preceding and succeeding chords.

Chords of the sixth, except when the bass-note is doubled
(as explained in the following paragraph) are not considered as
being definitely in either close or open position, as in the case of
the common chord; their position is regarded as being ambiguous, and as such it frequently happens that a chord of the
sixth intervenes between two common chords, one of which is in
close, while the other is in open position.

61. The bass-note of a chord of the sixth may be doubled (*a*) in L¹ generally ; (*b*) in II¹ frequently ; (*c*) when preceded by the same chord in root position ; (*d*) in L¹, II¹, IV¹ and VI¹, when two or more chords move conjunctly ; (*e*) when the doubled note is approached by conjunct movement and contrary motion ; (*f*) when the chord is preceded or followed by a triad on the same bass-note ; and (*g*) occasionally, for some particular reason, such as the avoidance of a bad harmonic progression.

The bass-note should *rarely*, if ever, be doubled when the third of the chord (i.e. the fifth of the root) is in the treble; and it should *never* be doubled if the bass is accidentally changed.

The doubled bass-note in all the above cases should, as a rule, be approached conjunctly, and if in the treble, it should be approached by contrary motion also, otherwise objectionable hidden octaves may arise.

62. The **best treble-note** in a chord of the sixth, as a general rule, is the sixth (the root), this being especially the case in II^1, III^1 and VI^1; in I^1, IV^1 and V^1, the third is also good in the treble; while, in L^1, either the octave, sixth or third may be placed in the treble. These rules hold good for both the major and the minor keys.

When two or more chords of the sixth occur in succession, the bass moving conjunctly, it is generally best to place *the sixth in the treble* and *the third in the alto* for each chord, and to let the tenor double *the treble and bass-notes alternately*, doubling the bass in L^1, II^1, IV^1, and VI^1 (§ 61, *d*). If desirable, however, the third may be placed in the tenor for each chord instead of in the alto; but the third should not be placed above the sixth in such a progression, unless one of the chords is L^1, as at *c*, § 63.

63. The diminished triad on L of the major key, as was seen in § 52, is rarely employed except in sequences; its first inversion, however, is an *important* chord; it generally occurs on an unaccented beat, and being a discord it must be resolved. It has two natural resolutions, namely (1) to I or I^1 (but never to I^2)when the sixth (L) must not be doubled, and (2) to III, when the sixth may be doubled. See also § 90, page 150.

In the minor mode, L^1 resolves on $I -$ and $I -^1$ only.

The dissonant note in the first inversion of a diminished triad, whether as L^1 in the major mode, or as L^1 or IIo^1 in the minor, is the third of the chord; and this note may, if necessary, be *doubled*, notwithstanding that it is a general rule in harmony that a dissonant note should *not* be doubled.   When the third in these chords is doubled, one third should rise and the other fall, each moving one degree only, as a rule, as at *a* and *b*.   The progression at *c*, where one third moves disjunctly to the tonic, is however, not forbidden.   In this progression, *c*, will be seen the one exception to the rule mentioned in § 62.

The consecutive fifths at (*b*), between the alto and tenor, do not produce a bad effect, the fifth above L being diminished.

64. The **best progressions** from common chords in root position to chords of the sixth occur when the bass falls a second or third ; the bass rising a second or fourth, falling a fourth or fifth, and rising a sixth from I and V, are also all good.   The bass rising a third or falling a sixth results in harmonic repetition, this effect is good, as has already been stated, when the first chord occurs on an accented beat.   It is rarely well to let the bass rise a fifth, otherwise it may be said that, practically speaking, all progressions from common chords to chords of the sixth are possible, for, even those which are not good when both chords are in root position, become acceptable when the second chord is taken in its first inversion.

The *best* progressions from chords of the sixth to common chords in root position, occur when the bass rises a second, that is to say, when the roots rise a perfect fourth ; the bass rising a third or fourth, or falling a fifth after I¹ and IV¹, and falling a second after L¹ and IV¹, are also all good.   The bass falling a third or rising a sixth results in harmonic repetition.   In no case should the bass fall a fourth or rise a fifth ; falling a sixth, after I¹ and IV¹, is possible but rarely good.

One chord of the sixth may be freely followed by another chord of the sixth if the bass moves a second. Disjunct movement between two chords of the sixth is generally not very good ; it is best when the bass falls a third; the bass falling a fourth and rising a fourth, or falling a fifth, after I¹ and IV¹, are also possible. It is rarely, if ever, good to let the bass rise a third or fifth, or move by any interval other than those already mentioned ; and, furthermore, in the case of disjunct movement the second chord should almost invariably fall upon an unaccented beat.

A common chord may be freely followed by a chord of the sixth on the same bass-note, and a chord of the sixth by a common chord on the same bass-note; the figuring for such progressions is 5 6 and 6 5 respectively, and it is generally best in each case to double the bass, and to let the moving notes appear in the treble. When a common chord is preceded or followed by a chord of the sixth on the note below, it is often conducive to a good melody to place the *third* of the common chord and the *root* of the chord of the sixth in the treble, the note common to the two chords being retained in an inner part, generally the tenor.

65. When a chord of the sixth is followed by a common chord, care must be taken to avoid objectionable **hidden consecutive fifths and octaves** between the *extreme* parts. Unless the roots of the two chords are a perfect fourth or fifth apart, and unless the treble move one degree only, hidden consecutives almost invariably produce *a bad effect*.

The progression at *a*, in the following example, is good , but that at *b* is very bad ; the hidden fifth *c*, and the hidden octaves at *d*, are disallowed ; at *e* the progression is bad, for L¹ should not resolve on IV (see § 63) ; the effect at *f* is good, the root being the same for both chords.

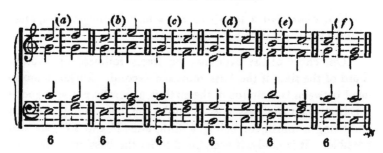

Hidden octaves are not altogether objectionable when the second chord occurs on an *unaccented* beat; thus, the progression at *g*, which is not good, is tolerated when it occurs as at *h*.

66. The chord of the sixth lends *much variety* to **cadences** occurring in the course of a composition; it is frequently employed as the first chord, and sometimes as the second chord of a cadence, in order to avoid the more conclusive effect which the chord possesses when in root position.

In **sequences** also, and especially in the dominant sequence, **the** chord of the sixth plays a most important part.

The chord of the sixth may well be termed the '*pons asinorum*' of Harmony. A thorough knowledge of this chord and of its treatment generally is of the utmost importance to the student, for, not only are the chords which have so far been considered, the only chords employed in strict counterpoint, but they may also be said to form the basis of all composition. As the present work is a treatise on harmony—not on counterpoint—the harmonization of melodies will be considered in the following chapter in conjunction with the chord of the six-four, in the first place, because it is advisable for the student to obtain a general knowledge of each of the inversions separately, and in the second place, because the conformation of a great number of melodies is of such a character that they cannot be satisfactorily harmonized without the use of the six-four chord.

SUMMARY.

§ 59. The inversions of the common chord.

> The effect of each inversion. Figures and symbols.

§ 60. The chord of the sixth.

> The bass-note, as a rule, should not be doubled.

§ 61. On doubling the bass-note.

> In L^1 generally, II^1 frequently, IV^1 and VI^1 occasionally.

§ 62. The best treble-note.

> 6 or 3 in primary triads, 6 only in secondary, and 8, 6 or 3 in L^1.

§ 63. The first inversion of the diminished triad on L.

> Two resolutions (a) L^1 to I or I^1 in both modes, and (b) L^1 to III in the major mode only.

§ 64. The best progressions to and from chords of the sixth.

> These progressions play a most important part in musical compositions; they should, as far as possible, be committed to memory.

§ 65. Hidden consecutive fifths and octaves.

> They are generally bad in effect, unless the roots move a perfect fourth or fifth, and the treble moves one degree.

§ 66. Cadences and sequences.

> The inverted cadence and the dominant sequence are of frequent occurrence. Triads and their first inversions, the only chords allowed in strict counterpoint, constitute the basis of all musical composition.

The following table may assist the student to remember the best treble-note, and, according to the underlining, when to double the bass in a chord of the sixth.

6 or 3	6 only	6 only	6 or 3	6 or 3	6 only	8, 6 or 3
I¹	II¹	III¹	IV¹	V¹	VI¹	L¹

EXERCISES.

1. Name the roots of the following chords, and in each case state whether the chord is major or minor.

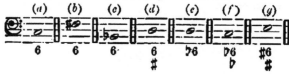

2. Write the first inversion of the tonic chord in the keys of A, E flat, F sharp minor and C minor; and the first inversion of the dominant chord in the keys of E, A flat, C sharp minor and F minor.

3. Complete the following passages by inserting the chords indicated by the symbols at the (vacant) beats marked a, b, c, d.

4. To each of the following chords add a preceding common chord, with roots falling a fifth, and a succeeding common chord with roots rising a fourth.

Add alto and tenor parts to the following :—

Add treble, alto and tenor parts to the following :—

7.

8.

9.

10.

11.

12.

13. Write the descending scales of A major and A minor (melodic form) in the bass, and harmonize them, employing a chord of the sixth for each degree except I.

14. Write, in the key-of F, the exercise of which the following is the symbolic analysis.

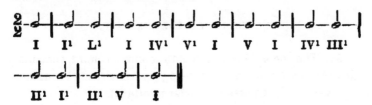

I   I¹   L¹   I   IV¹ V¹   I   V   I   IV¹ III¹

II¹ I¹   II¹ V   I

15. Write (a) in the keys of D major and G minor, the perfect and the imperfect cadences, employing a chord of the sixth followed by a common chord ; and (b) in the keys of B flat major and B minor, the same cadences, employing a common chord followed by a chord of the sixth.

16. Write a short sequence in the key of G, employing common chords and chords of the sixth alternately.

Exercises on the harmonization of unfigured basses and melodies will be found in Group II of the exercises at the end of the following chapter, when both inversions of the common chord may be employed. Additional exercises on chords of the sixth, if desired, may be obtained by re-writing the basses, Nos. 7 to 16, at the end of Chaper VI, and changing the chords, where practicable, from root position to first inversion ; in no case should the root of a chord be changed. The melodies also, Nos. 21 to 26, may now be harmonized, employing occasional chords of the sixth. Furthermore, the student would do well to compose several chants (single and double), hymn-tunes (such as No. 12, page 98), and other musical sentences ; with steady practice he will obtain a command of these concords, which will not only be invaluable to him in the study of counterpoint, but will also constitute the foundation of his musical compositions generally.

CHAPTER VIII.

THE CHORD OF THE SIX-FOUR.

67. The **second inversion** of the common chord, commonly called *the chord of the six-four*, being, as has already been stated (§ 59) a discord, requires particular treatment.

In counterpoint, which was the basis on which music was composed prior to the establishment of the laws of harmony, this chord, on account of its dissonant character, is *strictly forbidden*. It is indeed more than probable that harmony arose as a separate science from counterpoint partly on account of the use of this chord, and partly also on account of the free treatment of the dominant seventh, a chord which will be explained in the following chapter.

The second inversion is always *figured* $\frac{6}{4}$, hence the name; and its *root* is a fifth below the bass-note. The note to which especial attention must be directed is the fourth, the inverted root.

The second inversion of the common chord of C may be harmonized in any of the following ways.

The **symbol** for each of the above chords is I², or if necessary, I + ².

68. The most popular use of the chord of the six-four is on the *dominant*, preceding a common chord on the same bass-note or its octave, when it is called a **cadential** six-four; in this case, the bass-note should almost invariably be doubled; the fourth, as a rule, should be *approached conjunctly*; while the sixth should fall to the fifth, and the fourth to the third, in their respective parts.

69. In addition to the cadential six-four there are also, the **passing** six-four, (*a*) which usually occurs on II (V'); the **pedal** six-four, (*b*) which usually occurs on either I or V; and the **arpeggio** six-four, (*c*) which usually occurs on V.

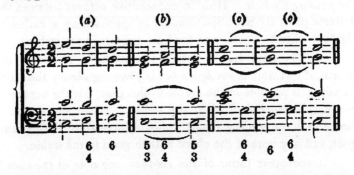

The passing and arpeggio six-fours may occur also upon any other degree of the scale, except alone IV; for the second inversion of a diminished triad is a forbidden chord.

In the following example, at *d*, a cadential six-four occurs on I, preceded by a passing six-four on II ; care must be taken in such progressions to *avoid consecutive fourths* between the bass and any of the upper parts. This chord (*d*) is sometimes called the **appoggiatura six-four.**

(*d*)

It is generally best to *double the bass-note* in all forms of the six-four; the *root*, however, may occasionally be doubled, especially in the arpeggio six-four; it is rarely advisable to double the sixth. In duple time, the cadential six-four should appear always on an *accented beat*; in triple time, it is best also on an accented beat, but it may fall on the second, though never on the third beat of the bar. The other forms of the six-four almost invariably occur on *unaccented beats*, especially the passing six-four. Hidden consecutive octaves between the extreme parts are not objectionable in approaching a cadential six-four when the octave of the bass appears in the treble.

70. The **best treble-note** in the cadential six-four is the fourth, if this note is *not heard in the preceding chord*; the sixth, however, is possible in the treble in this case, but the octave of the bass is generally bad in the treble. When the fourth *is* heard in the preceding chord it should be retained in the same part, and any note of the chord is then good in the treble.

In the other forms of the six-four, any note of the chord, speaking generally, is good in the treble; the fourth, however, *if approached disjunctly*, should as a rule be placed in the treble; and, if, so approached, it should be from *below*, and from the nearest possible note

71. The cadential six-four on V may be approached from any common chord in root position *which does not contain the leading-note*; also from the first inversion of any such chord, provided the bass does not move more than a third.   No definite rules can be laid down for approaching other forms of the six-four, suffice it to say that the upper parts should, as a rule, move as smoothly as possible to these chords; the fourth, especially, being approached conjunctly, when possible.

The cadential six-four naturally proceeds to a five-three on the same bass-note or its octave; the pedal six-four also usually proceeds to a triad on the same bass-note; the bass of a passing six-four should be quitted (as well as approached) conjunctly; and, in the arpeggio six-four, the bass naturally proceeds to another note of the same chord.   These progressions are illustrated in the above examples, § § 68 and 69.

72. Much use is made of the second inversion of the tonic chord (I²) in connection with both the perfect and the imperfect cadences, hence the name, cadential six-four.   An example of its employment in each of these cadences will be seen in the illustrative passage on page 123 ; at measure four, it occurs in the imperfect cadence, and at measure seven, in the perfect cadence.

The following passage exemplifies the use of the cadential six-four in sequences.

73. When a common chord is immediately succeeded by one or both of its inversions, instead of the latter being figured, a line, called the **line of continuation,** may be employed; this line is placed under the note or notes which *succeed* the chord, the harmony of which is to be continued.

By some modern authorities this line is placed under the bass-note of the chord the harmony of which is to be retained, as well as under the succeeding bass-notes; confusion, however, is liable to arise when this chord (the first chord) is figured; furthermore, the older plan avoids the necessity of adding a mark, of any kind whatever, to the bass-note of a common chord. No purpose is served by a change from which no advantage accrues.

The figure 1 under a bass-note implies that all the upper parts are to be in *unison*. The figure o, or the expression *tasto solo* (one key alone) implies that the upper parts are to rest, or, in other words, that the bass is not to be harmonized.

74. In harmonizing **unfigured basses,** the common chord and its inversions should be employed in accordance with the remarks in the following table. The common chord is here represented by the figure 5, in order to distinguish it from the chords of the sixth and six-four. This table holds good for both major and minor keys, if in the minor key the triad on II (being diminished), and that on III (being augmented), are avoided. IIo¹ (see § 63) may, of course, be employed; but III x¹ also should be avoided; while both IIo² and III x² are absolutely forbidden chords.

DEGREES OF THE SCALE.	FIGURES.	REMARKS.
I	5	Generally the best chord.
	6	Rarely good, except in a sequence of sixths.
	6 4	Good as pedal ; arpeggio and cadential also possible.
II	5	Good, if bass moves disjunctly.
	6	Good, if bass moves conjunctly.
	6 4	Good as passing ; arpeggio also possible.
III	5	Rarely good, except in a sequence.
	6	Generally the best chord.
	6 4	Very rarely good ; passing and arpeggio possible.
IV	5	Generally the best chord.
	6	Good, when the bass moves conjunctly, especially before a cadential six-four.
	6 4	Never good.
V	5	Generally the best chord.
	6	Rarely good, except in a sequence of sixths.
	6 4	Good in all forms, cadential especially.
VI	5	Good ; often the best chord.
	6	Generally good.
	6 4	Very rarely good ; arpeggio possible.
L	5	Good only in sequence (the diminished triad).
	6	Almost invariably the only good chord.
	6 4	Very rarely good ; passing and arpeggio possible.

If in a minor key, the major submediant occurs in the bass, it should be figured 6 ; and if the subtonic occurs, it also should be figured 6, when moving conjunctly ; when moving disjunctly, it suggests a modulation to the relative major key, and should therefore be treated as the dominant in that key.

75. In harmonizing **melodies,** it is necessary to consider the chord which is naturally suggested by each note as it occurs ; the root position or inversion of the chord being chosen in accordance with the harmonic progressions, as given in § § 38, 64 and 71 ; while the table in § 74 may also be found useful in this connection.

While it is scarcely possible to formulate any very definite rules for the harmonization of melodies, yet it may be said that it is generally advisable, in the first place, to decide upon and to work the *cadences,* together with the pre-cadential chords ; after this, a plan of the harmonic progressions should be arranged for the other notes of the melody ; and finally, the bass having been figured, the middle parts should of course be added.

The following table will be found valuable as a basis upon which simple melodies in general may be harmonized, when the common chord and its inversions alone are employed ; it holds good for both the major and the minor mode, with such exceptions for the minor mode as have already been mentioned. The first column under harmonic suggestions comprises the chords which should, as a rule, be employed ; the second column comprises chords which are equally good, and which may be regarded as alternative chords ; the third column comprises chords which may occasionally be employed, but which, speaking generally, are the least effective.

The table should be read as follows :—

The tonic in the melody, naturally suggests the tonic chord and its first inversion, and its second inversion when the melody suggests a cadential six-four ; also the submediant chord, and possibly the subdominant chord and its first inversion, and its second inversion as a pedal six-four. Etc.

THE DEGREES OF THE SCALE.	HARMONIC SUGGESTIONS.		
	PRINCIPAL.	ALTERNATIVE.	POSSIBLE.
I.	I and I¹, I² (a).	VI.	IV and IV¹, IV² (b).
II.	V and V¹ (c), V² (d).	II (e), II¹ (f).	L¹.
III.	I, I² (a).	VI.	III and III¹ (g, e).
IV.	IV and IV¹, IV² (b).	II (e).	L¹.
V.	I and I¹ (h), I² (i).	V and V¹ (j), V² (d).	III (g, e).
VI.	IV, IV² (b).	VI and VI¹.	II (g, e).
L.	V, V² (d).	L¹.	III (g, e).

(a) When the melody suggests a cadential six-four.

(b) As a pedal six-four.

(c) When the melody moves conjunctly, except before a cadential six-four.

(d) As a passing six-four.

(e) Not available in the minor mode.

(f) Before a cadential six-four.

(g) Very rarely.

(h) When the melody moves conjunctly.

(i) As a passing or pedal, and possibly as a cadential six-four.

(j) Before I, especially when it occurs upon an accented beat.

76. In harmonizing melodies, it is not sufficient to find a suitable chord for each note, nor is it sufficient to avoid consecutive fifths and octaves, and the other faults which have been enumerated from time to time; all of this may be accomplished and yet the result may be lacking in artistic effect.

The following simple melody, for example,

if harmonized as below

is far from satisfactory; at the same time, each chord is correct in itself, the harmonic progressions are correct, and the part-writing throughout is correct. The passage, however, is not a correct musical sentence; it is lacking in rhythm, and might well be termed 'harmonic meandering'; in other words, there is no middle cadence. Furthermore, the tonic chord is employed too frequently in root position, and, as the pre-cadential chord, it destroys to a certain extent the effect of the perfect cadence at the end.

Before commencing to harmonize a melody, it is advisable to mark the phrases, to insert the melodic symbols, and to decide upon the cadences. The above melody thus treated would appear as follows.

It may be taken as a general rule that the cadential six-four should be employed in connection with the perfect and the imperfect cadences, whenever the melody is of such a character that it may be correctly introduced. Although three notes of the melody have been included in each of the cadences, yet there are but *two* chords in effect in each case, for the $\frac{6}{4}$ and $\frac{5}{3}$ upon the same bass-note are regarded as one chord divided into two parts. In the following harmonization of the above melody, a pedal six-four is introduced in the first measure, a passing six-four in the second, and a cadential six-four in the fourth and seventh measures.

The above passage should be transcribed into the key of C minor, in which key it would be just as effective as in the key of C major.   It would be necessary to employ the correct key signature (three flats), and to place a natural before the note B, each time it occurs, otherwise the passage would remain as it stands.

The student is advised to compare the chords employed in this passage with the harmonic suggestions as given in the table in § 75. He would also do well to commit the passage to memory, to transpose it into other major keys, and to transcribe it into various minor keys.

Melodies in the minor mode which contain either the major submediant (+VI) or the subtonic (VII) of the scale necessitate the use of the additional triads (see § 57), or, in certain cases, a modulation to the relative major key.

The following examples illustrate the treatment of the subtonic in a descending passage.   At *a*, III+ is employed; at *b*, III+ with the parts moving sequentially; at *c*, III+, modulating to the key of E flat; at *d*, V-, with the parts again moving sequentially; at *e* and *f*, VII+[1], treated in two different ways.

The following examples illustrate the treatment of the major submediant in an ascending passage. At *g*, II - is employed; at *h* and *i*, +VIo[1] is treated in two different ways; at *j*, IV + is employed, but, as has already been said, the use of this chord in root position is not to be recommended; the examples at *k* and *l* are included as illustrations of progressions which should be avoided.

SUMMARY.

§ 67. The chord of the six-four.

The second inversion, unlike the first, is a discord.

§ 68. The cadential six-four.

The bass-note should be doubled, and the fourth, as a rule, approached conjunctly.

§ 69. Other forms of the six-four.

The passing, pedal, arpeggio and appoggiatura.

§ 70. The best treble-note.

The fourth, in the cadential six-four, if not heard in the preceding chord, is generally best in the treble ; if it is heard in the preceding chord, it should be retained in the same part.

§ 71. The best progressions to a cadential six-four.

No chord containing L should precede this chord, and the bass movement from a chord of the sixth should not be greater than a third.

§ 72. Cadences and sequences.

The cadential six-four is frequently employed in connection with both the perfect and the imperfect cadences, and with descending sequences.

§ 73. The line of continuation.

It indicates that one or more of the upper parts are to be retained over one or more of the succeeding bass-notes.

§ 74. Unfigured basses.

Table of chord characteristics.

§ 75. On harmonizing melodies.

First symbolize the melody, then determine the cadences with their pre-cadential chords, and lastly employ the harmonic suggestions as given in the table.

§ 76. The harmonization of melodies exemplified.

The student would do well to commit the examples to memory.

EXERCISES.

I.

1. Name the roots of the following chords, and in each se state whether the chord is major or minor.

2. Write the second inversion of the tonic chord in the keys of A, E flat, F sharp minor, and C minor; and the second inversion of the dominant chord in the keys of E, A flat, C sharp minor and F minor.

3. The chords marked *a*, *b*. *c*, *d* and *e*, in the following passage, are all second inversions; state the character of each whether cadential, passing or pedal, etc.

Add parts for alto and tenor to the following:—

Add parts for treble, alto, and tenor to the following :—

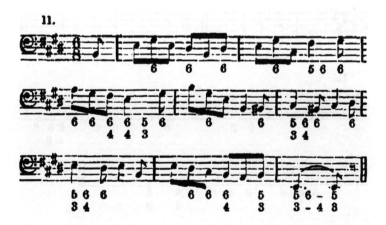

16. Give examples of the cadential, the passing, the pedal and the arpeggio six-four chords, (1) in the key of E flat, and (2) in the key of F sharp minor.

17. Write, in the key of G, the exercise of which the following is the symbolic analysis.

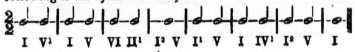

I V¹ I V   VI II¹ I³ V I¹ V   I IV¹ I² V   I

II.

Figure, and harmonize, the following basses.

18.

19.

20.

21.

22.

23.

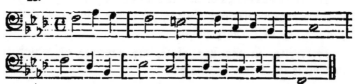

Harmonize the following melodies.

Clothe the following blank rhythms with harmony: each rhythm may be worked in both major and minor keys.

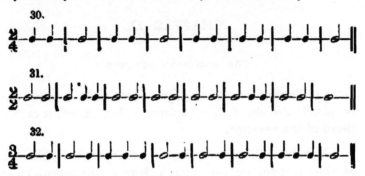

30.

31.

32.

Harmonize the following basses and melodies, introducing the additional triads of the minor mode.

33. Chant.

34.

35.

86.

37. Compose a double Anglican chant in the key of B.

38. Write a short passage in the key of G minor, introducing each form of the six-four.

CHAPTER IX.

77. To the triad on any degree of the scale, a *seventh* may be added; the chord then becomes a discord, and is called a **chord of the seventh.**

A chord of the seventh is named after the *root* of the triad on which it is constructed; thus, a chord of the seventh on the tonic is called a tonic seventh; on the supertonic, a supertonic seventh, and so on.

Chords of the seventh (and, as will be seen later, chords of the ninth) are termed **fundamental** discords, to distinguish them from certain other classes of discords.

The most important chord of the seventh is that formed on the *dominant*, the **dominant seventh** (see *a* and *b*); the other chords of the seventh are called *secondary* sevenths.

78. Chords of the seventh are figured $\frac{7}{5}$; this, however is usually contracted to $\frac{7}{3}$, or 7, according to the context.

The **symbol** for a chord of the seventh is formed by

adding the figure 7 to the symbol representing the *root* of the chord; thus, the symbol for the dominant seventh is V7.

V7, though theoretically a *primary* seventh, is always called a dominant seventh. The intervals of this chord, reckoning from the dominant, are

$$7 -$$
$$5$$
$$3 +$$
$$V$$

and since none of the secondary sevenths contain these same intervals, and moreover since IV and L, the distinctive notes of the scale, form part of the chord, it follows that the tonic of the key may always be readily determined, but the tonic only and not the mode, for V7 is exactly the same in both the major key and its tonic minor.

79. All *discords* require resolution. Resolution refers to the *succeeding* chord, the function of which is to *satisfy the ear* after the preceding element of dissonance. As a general rule, this resolution is effected by the part which takes the seventh *descending one degree* in the following chord. This is termed the natural resolution of the seventh, and it occurs (*a*) in the *principal* resolution, V7 to I (the perfect cadence), and (*b*) in the *deceptive* resolution, V7 to VI (the deceptive cadence).

In the principal resolution (with L in the treble) one of the chords must be *incomplete*, the fifth being omitted; it is indeed often advisable to omit the fifth in V7 when this chord occurs in the course of an exercise or a composition. When the fifth in V7 is omitted, the *root* should be doubled; for the seventh, being a note with a fixed progression, like L, must *never* be doubled.

In the deceptive resolution, on account of L proceeding in similar motion with the bass, it is necessary to double the third in VI; compare also § 47, *i*.

8o Any note of the chord may be placed in the treble, but, as a rule, and especially in the perfect cadence, the *third* of the chord (L) is the best treble-note.

When the seventh is in the treble, in the principal resolution, it is especially advisable to omit the fifth in V7, in order to secure a good position for the succeeding chord.

When L is in the treble, it should *invariably rise* to I; when in an inner part, L, in the principal resolution, may descend to V, if it is desirable for I to be complete; in the deceptive resolution, L may descend one degree in the major key, but in the minor, this progression would result in the skip of an augmented second.

As a general rule, however, L, in whatever part it may occur, should rise to I.

81. V7 may also proceed to I², as a pedal six-four, in which case it is again generally best to omit the fifth and double the root of the chord, as at *a*.

The progression V7 to I¹ (see *b*), is not allowed, for, in the first place, the note of resolution should rarely be doubled, and in the second place, if approached by similar motion, it must *never* be doubled. It is an inviolable rule that the octave (or unison) between any two parts, must not be approached by *similar* motion, *one part moving a second and the other a third*. This progression, V7¹ to I¹, has been employed as at *c*, where the seventh *rises* one degree, but this *exceptional* resolution of the seventh is only permitted when the *bass* proceeds to the note upon which the seventh naturally resolves.

The treatment of V7, as at *c*, in the above example is not recommended for the use of students.

82. In addition to the natural resolution of the seventh there are also the **stationary** and the chrcmatic resolutions. In the former, the part taking the seventh retains the same note in the succeeding chord, as at *a*, and frequently falls one degree naturally in one of the following chords, as at *b*; this latter is termed *deferred* resolution. In chromatic resolution, which will be considered more fully in the next chapter, the seventh rises a chromatic semi-tone, as at *c*, the succeeding chord being frequently another V7.

83. The seventh is said to be *ornamentally* resolved when it falls to the fifth or rises to the octave before proceeding to the note of resolution, as at *a*, *b*, *c* and *d*. Care must be taken in such cases to avoid the consecutives shown at *e*. The seventh may be introduced with ornamental effect after a common chord on V, as at *f* and *g*, the figuring, in this case, being 8 7. Here, again, it is necessary to avoid the consecutives shown at *h*, for the intervening seventh does not destroy the bad effect.

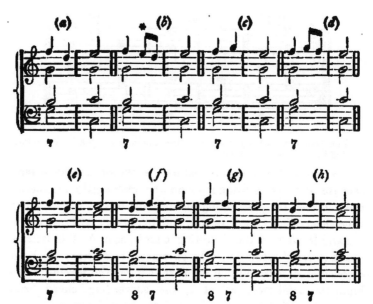

* This E is called a **Passing-note**, *i.e.*, a note not belonging to the chord, approached and quitted conjunctly, and
employed as an ornamentation.

Another form of ornamental resolution occurs when the
upper parts in V7 *move* while the bass remains stationary; in this
case the seventh may move *disjunctly*, provided that it is resolved
satisfactorily in the end by the part in which it appears last.

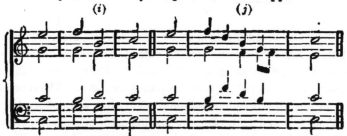

84. All progressions *to* V7 from common chords in root
position or first inversion are good, except from chords which

contain L, and excepting also VI[1]; these progressions, be it noted, are the same as those to the cadential six-four.

The best progressions *from* V7 are to I and VI; to I[2] and IV[1], occasionally employed; and, by chromatic resolution, to a V7 on the perfect fourth or fifth above or below.

The cadential six-four is often followed by V7; in this case the fourth should fall as usual to the third, but the sixth may either fall to the fifth or rise to the seventh.

85. In the perfect and deceptive *cadences*, as has already been shown, V7 plays an important part; in the imperfect cadence, however, it is rarely employed, for the second chord of a cadence should be a concord.

In *sequences*, V7 can rarely be introduced, except in the dominant sequence (roots rising a fourth or falling a fifth) when, by chromatic resolution, all the V7's in music may be successively introduced.

(a)

Similarly, roots rising fifths and falling fourths, as at *b* and *c*, also form a sequence which passes through the cycle of keys. It will be noticed that the treble in *a* proceeds chromatically *downwards*, while in *b* and *c* it proceeds chromatically *upwards*.

(*b*)

etc.

Or, the passage may be written thus:—

(*c*)

etc.

86. In harmonizing **unfigured basses and melodies**, the the seventh may be freely added to V, when the succeeding chord is either I or VI; except when V occurs as the second chord in the imperfect cadence. If V is followed by any chord other than I or VI, discretion must be employed, for whenever V7 is introduced it must, without exception, be *correctly resolved*.

The table for unfigured basses in § 74, and that for melodies in § 75, may be employed as the general basis upon which all simple diatonic melodies may be harmonized, (an unfigured bass being regarded as a melody for the lowest voice,) for the common chord itself is the basis of every other chord. Each new chord as it occurs will naturally necessitate some modification in these tables, but the general principles will remain the same throughout.

The most important change necessitated by the employment of V7, has reference to IV. When this note occurs in a melody and proceeds either directly or ornamentally to III, in addition to the chords given in the table in § 75, IV may be harmonized with V7. L and II, when proceeding to I, may also be harmonized with V7; if II rising to III is thus harmonized, it will necessitate the doubling of the third in I, which, though possible, is rarely advisable. V, when remaining stationary, may occur in the principal resolution, and when rising or falling to I, it may occur in the deceptive resolution.

SUMMARY.

§ 77. Chords of the seventh generally.
> Fundamental discords; primary and secondary sevenths.

§ 78. The dominant seventh.
> The figuring, the symbol, and the constituent intervals.

§ 79. The two natural resolutions
> The principal—V7 to I, and the deceptive—V7 to VI.

§ 80. The best treble-note.
> This is L, and when so placed it must rise to I.

§ 81. Variations of the resolution.
> V7 to I^1, bad; but V7 to I^2, good.   The note of resolution must not be doubled and approached by similar motion.

§ 82. Other resolutions.
> Stationary—V7 to IV^1, and chromatic—V7 to another V7.

§ 83. Ornamental treatment of the seventh.
> Passing notes, and change of position in the upper parts.

§ 84. The best progressions to V7.
> V7 should not be preceded by any chord containing L.

§ 85. Cadences and sequences.
> V7 is commonly employed as the first chord in the perfect and deceptive cadences ; and frequently employed in real sequences.

§ 86. Unfigured basses and melodies
> With the exception that IV may now be treated as forming part of V7, the tables given in §§ 74 and 75 should be employed as the general basis in this connection.

EXERCISES.

I.

1. Write the principal resolutions of the following chords.

2. Write the deceptive resolutions of the above chords.

3. Write, employing V7 for the first chord, the perfect cadence in the keys of B minor, F sharp minor, C sharp minor, G minor, C minor and F minor.

4. Write and resolve all V7's which contain the note D, placing D each time in the alto

5.

6.

The figure 1 under the first bass-note, indicates that the voices are to be in unison, see § 73.

Add treble, alto and tenor parts to the following:

7.

8.

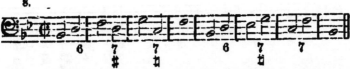

9.

10.

11.

13. Discover the mistakes in the following passage.

14. Exemplify the stationary resolution of the 7th employing the chord :—

15. Resolve the above chord chromatically, in two different ways.

16. Give two (or more) examples of the ornamental resolution of the 7th, employing the above chord.

II.

Harmonize the following unfigured basses.

17.

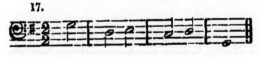

18.

19.

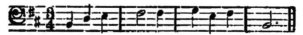

20.

21.

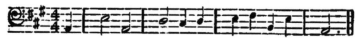

22.

Harmonize the following melodies.

23.

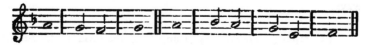

24.

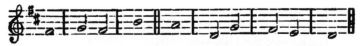

25.

26.

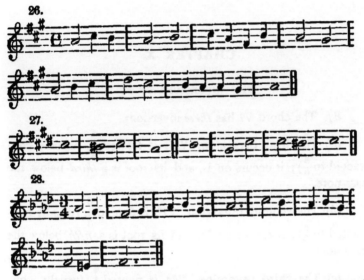

29. Clothe the following blank rhythm with harmony, in the key of E.

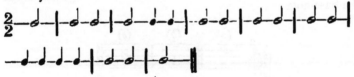

30. Write a short passage in the key of G minor.

CHAPTER X.

THE INVERSIONS OF V7.

87. The chord V7 has *three* inversions.

(*a*) The **first inversion**, V7^1, is figured $\frac{6}{5}$, (usually contracted to $\frac{6}{5}$); it occurs on L, and its root is a *third* below the bass-note.

(*b*) The **second inversion**, V7^2, is figured $\frac{6}{4}$, (usually contracted to $\frac{4}{3}$); it occurs on II, and its root is a *fifth* below the bass-note.

(*c*) The **third inversion**, V7^3, is figured $\frac{6}{4}$, (usually contracted to $\frac{4}{2}$); it occurs on IV, and its root is a *seventh* below the bass-note.

The general effect of the inversions is practically the same as when the chord is in root position. The seventh of the root, in the natural resolutions, must *fall one degree*, with one exception alone, (see § 89); while the third, L, should as a rule rise one degree to I.

88. The natural resolutions of the inversions of V7 are shown in the following example. At *a*, L being in the bass,

the chord of resolution is I; at *b*, the bass of the *four-three*
falls to I; it may, however, rise to I¹ (see § 89); at *c*, the seventh
of the root being in the bass, the chord of resolution is I¹.

Any note of these chords may be employed for the treble,
the root, perhaps, being the least interesting treble-note. It
will be seen that the bass-notes of the inversions move conjunctly in resolution; V7¹ rising one degree, V7³ falling one
degree, and V7² either rising or falling one degree.

Unlike the chord in root position, the inversions should as
a rule be *complete*; it is possible, though rarely advisable, to
omit the fifth of the root in the first and third inversions.

89. When the bass of a four-three *rises* one degree in the
chord of resolution, the third of the bass, that is to say, the
seventh of the root, *may also rise one degree*, in order to avoid
doubling the bass-note in I¹; this is termed the **exceptional
resolution** of the seventh.   In this case the *third* of the bass is
generally the *best treble-note*; if not in the treble, it should not
be a second below the (inverted) root, unless the root skips in
resolution, for the unison should not be approached by two
voices one of which moves a second while the other remains
stationary.

At *a*, the third of the bass descends naturally, doubling the
bass-note in the succeeding chord ; this is not incorrect, but it is
generally more effective to let the third *rise* one degree as at

b and *c*. At *d*, the resolution is not good, the third being below
the root which here remains stationary; with the root skipping,
however, as at *e*, the resolution is good. The consecutive fifths
at *b* do not produce a bad effect, the fifth above L being
diminished.

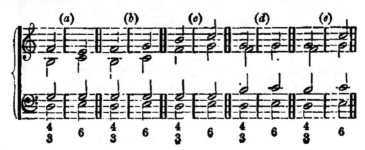

90. When the chord L¹ resolves on either I or I¹, as at *a*,
b and *c*, it is regarded as being an **Incomplete form** of V₇²,
and although L is the apparent root, yet V is the real root, or
generator, of the chord; the term generator signifying a note
from which a chord is derived, when that note is *not employed
in the chord*. It is generally best to double the bass-note in the
chord L¹ (see also § 63), as at *a* and *c*; the third, however,
notwithstanding its dissonant character, may *in this particular
case* be doubled, as has already been stated in § 63. When L¹
resolves on III, as at *d*, L itself is regarded as being the root,
and it may therefore be doubled, for the chord does *not possess
any dominant character* whatever.

91. Instead of *immediate* resolution, one inversion of the chord may be followed by another, or by the chord in root position, in which case the seventh may move disjunctly, and skips of even 4× and 7–, as at *a* and *b*, are possible; while the doubling of L in an arpeggio, passage, if sustained in one part, as at *c*, is not objectionable. The progression V7³ to V7, however, on account of the rising dissonance, (see *d*) is not allowed.

The ornamental resolutions, described in § 83, are equally available when the chord is inverted. V7³ is often introduced ornamentally after V, as *a passing note* in the bass, when, instead of the usual figuring, the line of continuation may be employed as at *e*, in the above example.

All the above resolutions may be transcribed to the tonic minor key; it will, of course, be necessary to raise accidentally the third of the root in V7, in every case, in the minor key.

92. The following example illustrates the deceptive resolutions of the inversions of V7; but these, it may be said, are not

in frequent use. At *a*, it is best to double the bass-note in VI^1; at *b*, L descends; it may, however, ascend, as at *c*, again doubling the bass-note in VI^1; at *d*, VI^2 is treated as a passing six-four, and occurs, therefore, on an unaccented beat.

The **stationary** resolution of the seventh is rarely employed in the inversions. In the following example, where the chord of resolution is treated as a cadential six-four on I, the effect is good.

93. The **chromatic** resolutions of V7 and its inversions are *most important.* One V7 may resolve on any other V7, provided that the roots of the two chords are *more than a tone* apart. There are, therefore, *seven* such resolutions; these are illustrated in the following example. It will here be seen that all parts move *conjunctly*, the notes which are common (both actually and chromatically) to the two chords, being invariably *retained in the same parts.* At *a*, *b* and *e*, the seventh descends naturally; at *c* and *f*, it ascends chromatically; at *g*, it remains stationary, and at *d*, it also remains stationary by an enharmonic change.

The above resolutions necessarily induce a modulation in every case. Modulation, to which reference has already been made in Chapter VI, will be treated of more fully in Chapter XI.

94. **The best progressions** *to* the inversions of V7 are from chords which do not contain L. The bass of V7², should, as a rule, be approached conjunctly; if L, in V7¹, is approached disjunctly, it should be from above, and if IV, in V7³, is so approached, it should be from below; for, in moving disjunctly to a note with a fixed progression, it is generally best to proceed to it from the *opposite* direction to that in which it resolves.

The best progressions *from* the inversions of V7 are the resolutions which have been given above.

The cadential six-four is often followed by V7³; in this progression both the sixth and fourth should descend one degree, as in the following example.

95. In **cadences**, with the exception of the perfect cadence, the inversions of V7 are rarely employed. In the

perfect cadence, in the place of V₇ in root position, an inversion produces a *less conclusive* effect, which is often desirable when the cadence is employed in the course of a composition.

The inversions of V₇ are frequently employed in real, but never in tonal sequences; the dominant sequence, especially, may be varied by the employment of the first and third inversions alternately; or by the employment of the root position and the second inversion alternately, as in the following examples.

Further examples of sequential progressions, of a modulating character, will be found in Chapter XVIII.

96. In harmonizing **unfigured basses**, V7¹, V7³ and V7⁰, respectively, may be employed when L, II and IV occur in the bass, provided that the succeeding chord admits of a *correct resolution*. When II is approached and quitted conjunctly, V7¹, or its incomplete form L¹, should invariably be employed; and it is especially desirable to employ V7³ when IV occurs in the bass preceded by V and followed by III. In other respects, the table, given in § 74, for harmonizing unfigured basses may be followed.

97. In harmonizing **melodies**, whenever a note which forms part of V7 occurs, either V7 or one of its inversions, speaking generally, may be employed. An exception, however, must be made in the case of both II and IV, when either of these notes *precedes a cadential six-four*; for, as has already been

stated (§ 71), no chord containing L should be employed in such a progression. Furthermore, it must be remembered that the second chord in the imperfect cadence should be V, or possibly V¹, and not V7, or one of its inversions.

In other respects, the table, given in § 75, for harmonizing melodies may be followed.

98. The following example illustrates the use of V7 and its inversions.

The student should bear in mind that in analysing chords, L¹, when it proceeds to either I or I¹, must invariably be regarded as the incomplete form of the second inversion of the dominant seventh, and that V (and not L) is the real root or generator of the chord.

SUMMARY.

§ 87. The inversions of the dominant seventh.

V7¹ occurs on L, V7² on II, and V7³ on IV.

§ 88. Their natural resolutions.

The bass-notes move one degree only; V7¹ rises, V7³ falls, and V7² either rises or falls.

§ 89. The exceptional resolution of V7³.

When the bass of V7³ rises one degree the seventh of the root may also rise one degree.

§ 90. The incomplete form of V7².

L¹ is so regarded when it resolves upon either I or I¹.

§ 91. Various treatments of the inversions V7.

One inversion followed by another before resolution.

§ 92. The deceptive resolution.

Sometimes, but not frequently employed; stationary resolution also of rare occurrence.

§ 93. The seven Chromatic resolutions.

One V7 may proceed chromatically to any other V7, provided the roots of the two chords are more than a tone apart.

§ 94. The best progressions to the inversions.

It is rarely good to approach these chords from any chord containing L; in the major mode, however, V7² may be approached from III.

§ 95. Cadences and sequences.

The inversions are rarely employed in connection with cadences, but frequently occur in real sequences, especially when the roots of the chords move a perfect fourth or fifth.

§ 96. Unfigured basses.

The inversions may be freely employed provided that the succeeding chord admits of correct resolution.

§ 97. On harmonizing melodies.

First symbolize the melody, then determine the cadences with their pre-cadential chords, and lastly employ the harmonic suggestions as given in § 75, introducing V7 and its inversions only when they can be correctly resolved.

§ 98. Illustrative example.

The student will do well to commit this passage to memory.

EXERCISES.

I.

1. Write the natural resolutions of the following chords, and in each case figure the bass and give the roots.

2. Explain the difference between the dominant seventh *on* B, and the dominant seventh *in* B; and write their inversions and resolutions.

3. Complete the following passage by inserting V7, or one of its inversions, at the (vacant) beats marked with an asterisk.

4. Treat the note C (second space in the bass) as the bass-note of four *different* chords of V7; figure and resolve each chord.

Add alto and tenor parts to the following:—

5.

Add treble, alto and tenor parts to the following:—

7.

8.

9.

10.

15.

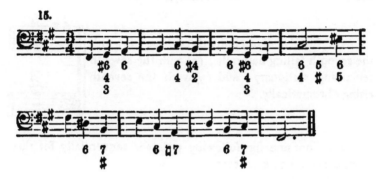

16.

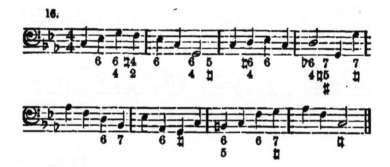

17. Explain the treatment of the supertonic sixth (L¹), in the following progressions.

18. Write a real sequence passing through all the major keys, employing V7ˢ and its natural resolution.

19. Resolve this chord three time; (1) with the seventh falling naturally; (2) with the seventh remaining stationary; and (3) with the seventh rising chromatically.

20. Continue the following passages sequentially for three more measures in each case.

21. Resolve this chord chromatically in seven different ways.

22. Write, in the key of G, the exercise of which the following is the symbolic analysis.

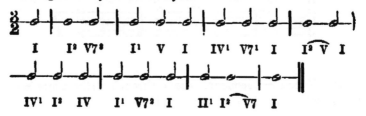

II.
Harmonize the following unfigured basses.

Harmonize the following melodies.

Clothe the following blank rhythms with harmony, each in both a major and a minor key.

35.

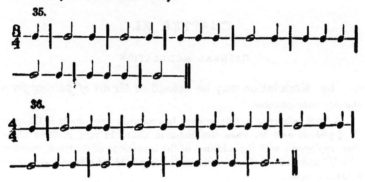

37. Compose a double chant in the key of E flat, employing a deceptive cadence for the first phrase, an imperfect cadence for the second, a plagal cadence for the third, and a perfect cadence for the last.

Add a figured bass and two upper parts to the following given inner parts; write in open score.

40. Write a short passage in the key of F sharp minor, introducing the inversions of V7, and some of the additional triads.

CHAPTER XI.

99. Modulation may be defined as *the art of passing from one key into another.*

A brief reference to this subject has already been made in Chapter VI, §§ 54, 55 and 56, when the common chord in root position alone was employed ; with the addition of the inversions of the triad, together with V7 and its inversions, a change of key may be effected in a more artistic manner.

When the new key is one of the attendant keys (see § 54), the modulation is said to be **natural ;** when otherwise it is said to be **extraneous.** Both natural and extraneous modulation may be effected either *gradually* or *suddenly*, and in certain cases (to be considered in a later chapter) by the enharmonic change of one or more notes in a chord, which is termed enharmonic modulation.

Modulation is generally effected by introducing V7 of the new key, which, resolving on the new tonic, *definitely establishes this key.*

Transition, a term sometimes employed instead of modulation, and sometimes signifying a modulation to an extraneous key, will here be employed only when a change of key is effected without the use of the dominant chord, or of any chord derived from the dominant.

100. In **gradual** modulation to an attendant key, *three* things are necessary, namely :—

1. The establishment of the *original key*.
2. The employment of one or more *ambiguous chords* *
   (see § 55).
3. The establishment of the *attendant key*.

---

* Sometimes termed equivocal or doubtful chords, for the reason that they do not belong definitely to either key.

These features will be seen in the following example, which illustrates a modulation from the key of C to its dominant—G.

The chords in this example may be analysed thus:—

a. I
b. V7¹ } Establishing the key of C.
c. I

d. { VI— in the key of C,
       or,
       II— in the key of G. } The ambiguous chord.

e. I²
f. V7 } Establishing the key of G.
g. I

Since the chord at *c*, in the above example, is the same as that at *a*, it is taken for granted that the tonic chord is sufficient to establish the original key. The cadential six-four at *e* is employed in order that V7 may fall on an unaccented beat, thus allowing the new tonic to appear on the accented beat, features which usually obtain when, as here, the modulation is *final*, that is to say, concludes (with a perfect cadence) in the new key. The number of chords absolutely necessary for gradual modulation may, therefore, be reduced to four; and when the original tonic is itself an ambiguous chord, as in the present case, the modulation may be effected by even three chords.

101. The following example illustrates gradual modulation from the key of C to each of its attendant keys.

The following example is a double Anglican chant in the key of A minor, with passing modulations to and through all of its attendant keys.

102. In sudden modulation there must be *no* ambiguous chord; in other words, the chord which precedes the new V7 must belong to the original key only; and this progression will therefore necessitate a chromatic change in at least one of the parts.

The following examples illustrate sudden modulation from the key of C to the key of G.

In the majority of cases the root progression to the new V7 will be *up or down a third*, as at *a*; a chromatic change from a minor chord to a V7 on the same root is shown at *b*; and *c* exemplifies the chromatic resolution of one V7 upon another, the roots moving a perfect fourth or fifth (§ § 82 and 93).

Modulation from a given major key to its relative minor or to the relative minor of the sub-dominant, also from a given minor to its sub-dominant, may be effected by the use of three chords only, viz.: the original tonic, and V7 and I – in the attendant key. In other cases an additional chord, usually IV or V, whichever will admit of chromatic movement in at least one of the parts, must be introduced after the original tonic.

103. The following example illustrates sudden modulation from the key of C to and through all of its attendant keys.

The following example illustrates sudden modulation from the key of A minor to each of its attendant keys.

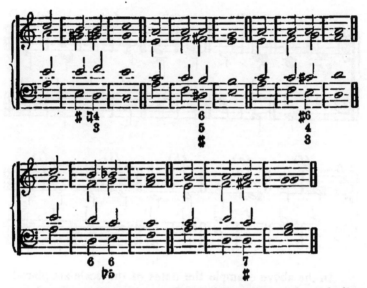

104. In harmonizing **unfigured basses and melodies,** modulations to attendant keys may often be effected in simple diatonic passages ; especially when a note falls one degree from a weak to a strong beat.

The melodic progression II to I, which naturally suggests the perfect or the deceptive cadence, may be treated as IV to III in the relative minor key, as at *a* ; III to II, which often suggests the imperfect cadence, may be treated as II to I in the relative minor of the subdominant, as a *b* ; IV to III, which often suggests the plagal, and sometimes the authentic (perfect) cadence, may be treated as at *c* ; two different treatments of V to IV are shown at *d* and *e*; two different treatments of VI to V (a progression which often suggests a plagal cadence) are shown at *f* and *g* ; L to VI may be treated as II to I in the relative minor, as at *h* ; and I to L, which often suggests an imperfect cadence, may be treated as IV to III in the dominant, as at *i*; or as VI to V in the relative minor of the dominant, as at *j*.

In the above example the notes of the scale are placed in the melody in each case; they may, however, be placed in the bass or indeed in any other part, while V7 may be employed in any suitable inversion, as well as in the root position.

Modulations of a similar character may be effected in the minor mode: if VII (the subtonic) is employed, it is frequently treated as V in the relative major.

When the melody *rises* one degree, modulations are not as readily suggested as (in the above examples) when it *falls* one degree. Special reference, however, should be made to the melodic progression II to III, which is often harmonized as at *k*. This particular progression, although it may be regarded as  a modulation to, and as an imperfect cadence in the key of the relative minor, is sometimes employed as a cadence in the key of the tonic; in which case, the second chord (the symbol for which would be III+) is regarded as a chromatic concord, and the progression itself is often called the Phrygian cadence.

105. Extraneous modulation will be considered in detail in Chapter xviii. This subject, however, has already received some attention in connection with thè chromatic resolutions of V7 (Chapter x, § 95). Gradual modulation to an extraneous key may be effected by the employment of natural modulation to one or more intermediate keys; modulation of this character is said to be Compound. Compound modulation, therefore, consists of one or more passing or *transient* modulations, followed by a final or *permanent* modulation to a more or less distant key.

106. A modulation from a given major key to its tonic minor, or from a given minor to its tonic major, may be effected by the use of the V7 common to both keys; such a modulation, although strictly speaking extraneous, is frequently employed in connection with natural modulation. The keys of C major and E major, for example, may be connected by identically the same chords as the keys of C major and E minor, (see § 101, page 168), with the exception that the final chord must be major, instead of minor. Upon this principle, and by means of compound modulation, the most distant keys may be connected by the chords employed in natural modulation. Thus, in the following example, a modulation is made from the key of C major to that of F sharp major, first by proceeding to the tonic major of A minor, and thence to the tonic major of F sharp minor.

The student would do well to commit to memory the modulations from the key of C to each of its attendant keys, as given in §101 ; and to symbolize the chords, for the same symbols, as employed there, may also be employed in modulating from any major key to its attendant keys. In the above example, it will be seen that the ambiguous chord in proceeding from A major to F sharp minor is the same as in proceeding from C major to A minor. The cadential six-four, it may be said, is employed so that the new V7 may appear on an unaccented beat, thus allowing the perfect cadence to occur in the normal manner.

107. In connection with this subject of modulation, and changing from one key to another, it may be stated, that, *theoretically*, there is but one key, and one alone, in music, namely, the key of the tonic ; it has two forms, the major mode and the minor mode. The normal pitch of this tonic is represented by the note C, but for practical purposes, either from an instrumental or a vocal consideration, or for some other reason (or perhaps for no particular reason at all), the pitch of this tonic may be represented by any other sound in music ; but whatever note, other than C, is taken for the tonic, the chords, the harmonic progressions and the whole paraphernalia of the key bear exactly the same relationship to that tonic as though that tonic were C· All other major keys, in fact, may be regarded as transpositions from C major, and all other minor keys as transpositions from C minor ; but it is not practicable to *transpose* music from a major key into a minor key, nor vice versa, for by transposition is understood the reproduction of *exactly the same effect* at a different pitch, and a minor chord can never possess exactly the same effect as a major chord. Music, in certain cases, may be *transcribed* from a major to a minor key, or vice versa, but this can only be effected when the harmonic progressions are of the simplest character.

Unfortunately the term "transposition" is sometimes employed in this connection, but "transcription" is undoubtedly the correct term.

108. At this stage in the study of Harmony, the student will do well to take a glance at the past, and see what he has so far accomplished, also to look into the future, and learn what there is yet in store for him. Having once mastered the common chord, the only concord in music, the remainder of his career in

the realm of harmony will be devoted to the study of discords. Discords are of two kinds, essential and unessential. To the former class belong chords of the seventh and ninth, discords derived from a root by super-imposing a series of thirds, and commonly called Fundamental discords; while to the latter class belong two forms of discords, those known as Suspensions and those formed by the use of Auxiliary notes. After conquering the diatonic concords and discords, the attention of the student is directed to the chromatic element in harmony, which also comprises both concords and discords, and with which is included the subject of enharmonic modulation. Such, then, are the chords which are treated of in the science of Harmony (§ 32); and to understand them, to know how to introduce them, how to resolve them, and how to employ them with good effect, and to be able to recognize them and to appreciate their treatment in the works of the great classical masters, should be the constant aim of every earnest student.

109. To obtain a knowledge of the chords employed in Harmony, however, should not be the only object in view; the student should endeavour to make some practical use of his theoretical acquirements, that is to say, he should compose music. Even with the present limited means at his disposal, he has sufficient material to compose hymn-tunes, of a very high order of merit, and the hymn-tune may well be regarded as the acorn from which develops the mighty oak of all musical composition. In his early attempts the student should not try to be original, he should rather try to imitate what others have done before him; let him imitate as a student, and originate as a composer. Having mastered the hymn-tune, the student probably will crave for higher types of composition, he should then turn his attention to the study of Form in Music, and (with the assistance of a teacher) may attempt to write a short Anthem or Part-song or perhaps a March or Minuet. Compositions of this character will lead him on gradually to more advanced types, such as the Sonata and the Cantata; and, finally, to the very highest types of all, the Opera, the Oratorio and the Symphony.

SUMMARY.

§ 99. Natural modulation.

Two kinds—gradual and sudden. The student should read § § 54, 55 and 56, before commencing to study this chapter.

§ 100. Gradual modulation.

The importance of the ambiguous chord, see also § 55.

§ 101. Examples of gradual modulation.

(a) From the key of C to each of its attendant keys; (b) from the key of A minor to and through each of its attendant keys.

§ 102. Sudden modulation.

No ambiguous chord; a chromatic change necessary.

§ 103. Examples of sudden modulation.

(a) From the key of C to and through each of its attendant keys; (b) from the key of A minor to each of its attendant keys.

§ 104. Unfigured basses and melodies.

The simplest diatonic passages frequently contain modulating possibilities; in other respects basses and melodies may be treated as explained in the preceding chapters.

§ 105. Compound modulation.

Passing through one or more intermediate keys.

§ 106. The tonic major and minor modes.

By their use the most distant keys may be connected on the principles of natural modulation.

§ 107. The key of the tonic.

Modulation, change of key; transposition, change of pitch; transcription, change of mode.

§ 108. The chords employed in Harmony.

Concords and discords, diatonic or chromatic; essential discords, derived from a root; unessential discords, formed by the use of suspensions and auxiliary notes.

§ 109. The composition of music.

Ability to compose a hymn-tune the first step on the road which leads to the highest types of musical composition.

EXERCISES.

1. Complete the following passages, in either $\frac{2}{2}$ or $\frac{3}{2}$ time, modulating *gradually* in each case to the key indicated.

(a) G+ to E– (b) F+ to A–   (c) A+ to D+

(d) E♭+ to B♭+   (e) E+ to F♯–

2. Figure and harmonize the following passages, modulating *suddenly* in each case to the key indicated.

(a) F+ to D–   (b) D+ to E–   (c) B♭+ to F+

(d)   A+ to C♯–   (e)   E♭+ to A♭+

3. Modulate gradually, employing not more than four chords in each case, (a) from the key of D, and (b) from the key of G minor, to each of their attendant keys, (ten exercises).

4. Modulate suddenly, employing as few chords as possible in each case, (a) from the key of B-flat, and (b) from the key of B minor, to each of their attendant keys, (ten exercises).

5. Modulate from A to C-sharp minor suddenly and return to A gradually.

6. Modulate from C minor to A-flat gradually and return to C minor suddenly.

7. Compose a single Anglican chant in the key of E, introducing a modulation to the dominant.

8 Clothe the following blank rhythm with harmony in the key of F minor, introducing a modulation to the relative major.

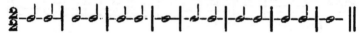

The plan of chords adopted in the example in § 100 may be followed in working this exercise.

9. Compose a double chant in the key of B; modulate to G sharp minor in the first phrase, to F sharp major in the second, to E in the third, and return to B in the last.

10. Write a continuous passage of modulation commencing in the key of D flat and passing to and through all its attendant keys.

11. Modulate gradually (a) from F sharp to D flat, and (b) from G flat to C sharp, making the enharmonic change at the ambiguous chord.

12. By means of the chromatic resolution of one V7 to another (see § 93) modulate (a) from C to F, (b) G to D, (c) F to A flat, (d) D to F sharp, (e) B flat to G, (f) A to F, and (g) E flat to A.

II.

Harmonize the following unfigured basses, introducing modulations as indicated.

13

Harmonize the following melodies, introducing judicious modulations.

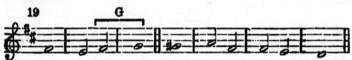

APPENDIX.

SYMBOLS.

The symbols employed in the present work by which notes and chords are represented *without the use of words*, may be regarded as forming a system of musical stenography.*

Symbols are of two kinds, namely:—

Melodic, representing a note, and

Harmonic, representing a chord.

Four factors are employed in the formation of these symbols, namely, (1) certain Roman numerals, (2) the Arabic numbers, 1, 2, 3, etc., up to 9, (3) certain signs, and (4) the marks ' and ‚.

(1) The Roman numerals, sometimes preceded by one of the signs (3) are employed to indicate notes, whether diatonic or chromatic.

(2) The Arabic numbers are employed to represent intervals and, when they appear in small type (like the sign for square and cube, etc., in mathematics) to represent the inversions of chords.

(3) The signs, four in number are, +, -, × and o; these are employed to indicate respectively the terms, 'major', 'minor,' 'augmented' and 'diminished.'

(4) The mark ' is employed to represent a suspension; thus ‚ for a falling, and thus ‚ for a rising suspension.

The symbols for intervals are formed by placing the sign representing the particular name *after* the Arabic number representing the general name of the interval.

---

* The term 'symbol' which is here used, it is believed, for the first time in connection with the subject of harmony, was suggested by the use of the same word in chemistry, astronomy, etc, where it is employed (as in the present work) to indicate a certain significant mark—letter, figure or sign—which stenographically represents the name of *something* under consideration. The derivatives, *symbolic* (having reference to symbols) and *symbolise* (to mark with symbols) are occasionally also employed in this work.

Thus, for example : —

     2 +   indicates a major second ;
     3 -   "   a minor third ;
     4 ×   "   an augmented fourth ;
     5 ○   "   a diminished fifth.

The sign + indicates the term ' perfect,' when it is employed after the numbers 4, 5 and 8.

The student should call each symbol by its proper name ; for example, a major second should not be read as ' two plus,' nor a minor third as ' three minus,' etc.

The melodic symbols for the various degrees of the major and minor scales, the latter in its harmonic form, are shown in the following example.

It will be seen that the same symbol is employed for the mediant in both keys ; when it is desirable to distinguish between the major and minor mediants, the signs + and - respectively are placed before the symbol, thus, +III and -III. The same may be said of the two submediants. In the melodic form of the minor scale, the submediant in ascending is, therefore, +VI, while in descending it is -VI. The technical name (employed in the present work) for the seventh degree in the descending form of the minor scale is ' subtonic ' ; the symbol employed for this note is VII.

The symbol L is employed for the leading-note instead of VII (as might have been expected) because in the first place, it is easier to write and, what is frequently an important consideration, it occupies less space than VII ; and, in the second place, because a distinctive symbol more readily directs the attention of the student to the characteristics of the note (See page 14). A point of small importance but one not unworthy of a passing notice is to be seen in the number 50 which is the numerical significance of the Roman numeral L, while 5o (as was shown above) is the symbol for the interval of the diminished fifth, an interval invariably associated with the leading-note in both the major and minor modes.

The technical name (or symbol) for each degree of the scale should invariably be employed in preference to the alphabetical name ; for the alphabetical name varies with each new scale but the technical name always remains the same. Furthermore, it may here be said, that each degree of the scale possesses a certain individuality peculiar to itself, which may be termed its *æsthetic character* ; e. g., I—Constancy, II—Desire, III—Ease, IV—Faith, V—Gladness, VI—Adversity and L—Brightness. These terms, which are suggestive only of the æsthetic character of each note, have been chosen so as to be easily remembered by the student ; the initial letters, it will be seen, form the scale of C.

The following table comprises the melodic symbols for the notes of the modern enharmonic scale of C (See page 34) ; together with the technical names employed (in the present work) for the notes of this scale.* The alphabetical name and tonal character of each note are also included. The table should be read upwards.

ALPHABETICAL NAME.	MELODIC SYMBOL.	TECHNICAL NAME.	TONAL CHARACTER.
B.	L	Leading-note.	Diatonic.
B flat.	VII	Subtonic.	Perfect chromatic.
A.	+VI	Major submediant.	Diatonic.
A flat.	−VI	Minor submediant.	Imperfect chromatic.
G sharp.	×V	Hyper-dominant.	" "
G.	V	Dominant.	Diatonic.
F sharp.	×IV	Inter-dominant.	Perfect chromatic.
F.	IV	Subdominant.	Diatonic.
E.	+III	Major mediant.	"
E flat.	−III	Minor mediant.	Imperfect chromatic.
D sharp.	×II	Hyper-supertonic.	" "
D.	+II	Major supertonic.	Diatonic.
D flat.	−II	Minor supertonic.	Imperfect chromatic.
C sharp.	×I	Hyper-tonic.	" "
C.	I	Tonic.	Diatonic.

*It is with a feeling of much diffidence that certain new technical names are here introduced, but at the same time it is under the conviction that they will supply a long-felt want,

The perfect chromatics—the inter-dominant and the sub-tonic—are so called because they are employed in chord construction in one form only; the imperfect chromatics, by enharmonic change, are employed in both forms.

The notes G flat and A sharp are sometimes employed as chromatic auxiliary notes, but they have, it may here be said, no harmonic relationship with the key of C. For the sake of completeness, should it at any time be necessary to refer to such notes, the technical names, Hypo-dominant (oV) and Hyper-submediant (x VI) may be respectively employed.

Equal temperament, that is to say, the division of the octave into twelve equal semitones, is the fundamental principle of all that appertains to modern music. The above scale, it will be seen, contains two distinct kinds of semitones—the diatonic and the chromatic—but these must be regarded as being absolutely equal in point of size. Scientifically, the ratio of the former is as 15 : 16, and that of the latter as 24 : 25; in other words, theoretically D flat (for example) is of slightly higher pitch than C sharp: in equal temperament however, these two notes—D flat and C sharp—are tempered, that is to say, tuned into one and the same note. This theory of equality can alone justify the chromatic progressions and the enharmonic modulations of modern composers.

Harmonic symbols are formed from melodic symbols by the addition of numbers, signs and marks, according to the character of the chord; the melodic symbol indicates the root of the chord.

The triads as they occur in the keys of C major and minor are shown in the following example.

C Major.

I+   II –   III –   IV+   V+   VI –   Lo

C Minor.

I-   IIɒ   III ×   IV-   V+   VI+   Lo

The signs, + and –, etc,. as a matter of fact, are frequently omitted, being understood; the student, however, should employ them at first, and indeed until he is perfectly familiar with the character of the various triads. In reading the symbols, the student should be careful to employ the correct technical term; for example, I+ should be read as 'the tonic major triad (or chord),' and not as ' one plus.'

The following example illustrates some of the chromatic triads (in the key of C) with their symbols.

The symbols for the first and second inversions of triads are formed by placing the small figures 1 and 2 respectively, after the sign indicating the character of the chord; thus, $I+^1$, the first inversion of the tonic major chord, and $I-^2$, the second inversion of the tonic minor chord. The following example illustrates the first inversion of the triad of C, as it occurs in seven different major keys.

The sign 'o,' it will be seen, is omitted after the symbol L; this is invariably the case when L^1 has a dominant character and resolves on I or I^1; when it resolves upon III –, the sign 'o' should be added, thus, Lo^1.

The following example illustrates the symbols employed for the chords of the seventh in most frequent use, in both C major and C minor. The sign + is usually omitted after V, as this chord is invariably major.

The symbols for the inversion of chords of the dominant seventh are formed thus $V_7{}^1$, $V_7{}^2$, and $V_7{}^3$.

The symbols for the chords of the dominant ninth are V_{9+} (or simply V_9) and V_{9-}. L_7 and L_7o are treated as distinct chords, they are not regarded as being $V_{9+}{}^1$ and $V_{9-}{}^1$ respectively; in the latter chords the dominant is always present while in the former it is never present.

The following example illustrates the formation of symbols in connection with suspensions.

(a)   The tonic chord with the third suspended.
(b)   The dominant seventh with the fifth suspended.
(c)   The tonic chord with the octave sub-suspended.
(d)   The first inversion of the tonic chord with the bass suspended.
(e)   The third inversion of the dominant seventh with the third and fifth suspended.
(f)   The tonic chord with a triple suspension.

When the suspension is in the bass, the mark ' is placed before the Roman numeral.

Pedal chords and pedal passages are represented by the Roman numeral indicating the pedal note, followed by a line of continuation placed under, or in the case of an inverted pedal placed over, the symbols representing the chords employed in connection with the pedal note.

In the case of ambiguous chords, the second symbol is placed under the first.

Sufficient, it is hoped, has now been said, to explain the theory upon which the symbols in general are constructed and employed. The symbols for other chords, both diatonic and chromatic, will be given as the chords severally occur in the course of the work.

The following passage exemplifies the employment of symbols in connection with modulation.

The above symbols should be read as follows:—

(*a*) The dominant seventh.

(*b*) Tonic (major) chord.

(*c*) Leading seventh (or minor seventh on leading-note) on tonic pedal.

(*d*) Tonic chord with fifth and third suspended, end of pedal.

(*e*) Augmented triad on tonic.

(*f*) Sub-dominant (major) chord.

 g) First inversion of dominant seventh, in G major.

(*h*) Tonic (major) chord with octave suspended.

(*i*) Diminished seventh on leading-note, generator E, in A minor.

(*j*) Tonic (minor) chord, changing to mediant (minor) chord, in F major.

(*k*) Second inversion of dominant seventh.

(*l*) Tonic (major) chord, with octave sub-suspended and third suspended.

(*m*) First inversion of dominant chord, changing to first inversion of tonic chord, in C major.

(*n*) First inversion of supertonic seventh.

(*o*) Dominant sixth and seventh.

(*p*) Tonic chord.

From the above analysis, it will be seen that both time and space are materially saved by the employment of symbols, irrespective of the convenience derived from having the name of each chord immediately under its own bass-note. It can with confidence be affirmed that were the advantages to be derived from the use of symbols generally known, the system would without doubt be generally adopted.

INDEX.

Lightning Source UK Ltd.
Milton Keynes UK
UKHW020717250822
407828UK00007B/985